Oli Forsyth

Kings

T0353539

Bloomsbury Methuen Drama
An imprint of Bloomsbury Publishing Plc

B L O O M S B U R Y
LONDON • OXFORD • NEW YORK • NEW DELHI • SYDNEY

Bloomsbury Methuen Drama

An imprint of Bloomsbury Publishing Plc

Imprint previously known as Methuen Drama

50 Bedford Square	1385 Broadway
London	New York
WC1B 3DP	NY 10018
UK	USA

www.bloomsbury.com

**BLOOMSBURY, METHUEN DRAMA and the Diana logo
are trademarks of Bloomsbury Publishing Plc**

First published 2017

© Oli Forsyth, 2017

Oli Forsyth has asserted his right under the Copyright, Designs
and Patents Act, 1988, to be identified as author of this work.

British Library Cataloguing-in-Publication Data
A catalogue record for this book is available from the British Library.

ISBN: PB: 978-1-3500-6208-5
ePDF: 978-1-3500-6209-2
ePub: 978-1-3500-6210-8

Library of Congress Cataloging-in-Publication Data
A catalog record for this book is available from the Library of Congress.

Series: Modern Plays

Cover image © Guy J. Sanders

Typeset by Mark Heslington Ltd, Scarborough, North Yorkshire

To find out more about our authors and books visit *www.bloomsbury.com*. Here you
will find extracts, author interviews, details of forthcoming events and the option
to sign up for our *newsletters*.

Kings

In memory of Mary,
Dedicated to Emma,
And, as always, for N.E.O.N.

Smoke & Oakum Theatre was founded by artistic director Oli Forsyth as a new writing company in 2013. Since then they have produced six shows that have gone on in front of thousands of people at venues all over the UK. Of the plays they have created four have been published, the rights to which have been bought by drama schools and companies across the country. Smoke & Oakum shows cover a range of topics, from boxing to rave culture, and always have the same mix of urgency and crackling dialogue that led David Byrne to label them 'One of the best new companies around'.

Cast & Creatives

Hannah	**Emma James**
Caz	**Madeleine MacMahon**
Ebi	**Andy McLeod**
Bess	**Johanna Allitt**
Man	**James Barbour**

Written and Directed by Oli Forsyth
Produced by Smoke & Oakum Theatre

Designer	Erin Green
Sound Design	Diarmaid and Darragh Browne
Lighting Design	Matthew 'Lux' Swithinbank
Stage Manager	James Barbour
Image Design	Guy J. Sanders
Construction	Keith Millar
Website and Brand Design	Emma Forsyth
Script Consultant	Stewart Pringle
Casting	Lucy Hagan-Walker
Press	Borkowski PR

Thanks

Special thanks must go to David Byrne and the team at
New Diorama for their continued support of Smoke & Oakum
Theatre, Sam Carrack for all his brilliant work, former cast
members Helen Belbin and Isaura Barbé-Brown, Julia Tyrrell,
Dom O'Hanlon, Beth Moss. Gregor Cubie, Fenella Dawnay,
Sir David and Primrose Bell, Tom Stoppard, Moira Buffini and
Michael Frayn, The Mackintosh Foundation, the Peggy Ramsay
Foundation, and finally our partners Centrepoint
and Lisa Maxwell.

Kings

Characters

Ebi, *later thirties*
Bess, *later thirties*
Hannah, *nineteen*
Caz, *early thirties*
Man

Scene One

Lights up on the camp. It's situated under a railway arch and is a semi-permanent collection of tents, littered cans and sandwich packets, some personal effects, bags, spare coats, etc. Centre stage is an old oil drum in which a fire flickers.

Standing around the fire is **Ebi** *who has been sleeping rough for some time. He is resigned to the homeless way of life and has the weary, slow movement of someone who spends a lot of time trying to conserve their energy.*

Centre stage, passed out under a sleeping bag and relatively unnoticeable is **Hannah**.

Enter **Bess**. *She has been sleeping rough for a number of years and shows the strain of such an existence. She's almost constantly cold, hungry and in danger of being moved on. Accordingly her movement, and temper, are sharp and aggressive.*

She enters the camp cold and wet from the downpour going on outside. She strides straight across the stage, removing her wet coat and shoes before diving into the furthest tent. Seconds later she emerges with a bottle of water and dry clothes which she quickly puts on. Eventually she joins **Ebi** *at the fire.*

Ebi   So . . . how was it?

Bess *hocks deeply and spits into the flames.*

Ebi   That bad?

Beat.

Ebi   Well, it's a tough spot.

Bess (*sullen*)   It's not.

Ebi (*laughing*)   I think it is. I think it's a very tough spot. Be lucky to get (*Looking over, guessing.*) £10 there.

Bess's *frustration grows.*

Ebi   Well, I hate to say I told you so.

Bess   Do you, Ebi? Do you? Seem to be enjoying yourself a lot.

Ebi   Well, I did say this morning. I told you not to waste your time and that it was a tough spot, but did you listen? No. That's why you're mardy.

Bess   I'm not mardy.

Ebi   No, you're cool you are. Cool like a cucumber. Got the solid calm of a woman with £50 in her pocket.

Bess   Maybe I do.

Ebi   Maybe. (*Beat.*) Unlikely to be £50 there though cos, like I said, the high street's a tough spot.

Bess   It's not a fuckin' tough spot, alright? It's not.

Ebi   So how'd you do?

Bess   I was doing fine.

Ebi   Oh yeh?

Bess   Yeh. Got the right place.

Ebi   Where's that then?

Bess   The stretch between McDonald's and the NatWest.

Ebi   Just before the station?

Bess   Yep.

Beat.

Ebi   That is a good spot. Surprised you had it to yourself.

Bess   Well . . .

Ebi   Here we go. Get booted did you?

Bess   How dare you? Booted? Me?

Ebi   Sorry, didn't mean to offend a woman of your standing in the community. (*Beat.*) But you got booted?

Bess   No, I did not 'get booted'. Just had to share was all. Some woman in a burka planted her fat arse right across the street from me.

Ebi *chuckles.*

Ebi   Who was she?

Bess   Don't know, never seen her before.

Ebi   Probably fresh off the boat. Should have said something.

Bess   I did. Told her I was here first and to find her own bloody spot.

Ebi   And?

Bess   Didn't have a word of English apparently. Not one word. Had a fuckin' board with her life story written on it mind, but all I got was a blank face.

Ebi   Should have booted her.

Bess   Oh that would've done me a world of good, Ebi. Good thinking. Booting a charity case in broad daylight. I'd have been raking it in after that.

Ebi   So you lost out to her did you?

Bess   No. I was doing plenty fine, even with her there.

Ebi   So what happened?

Beat.

Bess   Some fuckin' – kid – with a fuckin' guitar starts up not 10 metres from me.

Ebi   Ah, game over.

Bess   Had a tambourine on his foot and a harmonica in his mouth. Fuckin' one-man band playing nineties classics. What was I going to do with that?

Ebi   Should have had a word.

Bess   I did. Asked him to shift down a bit but he just kept playing away. I'm raging away at the little shit, turning blue like, and all I get coming back at me is an acoustic rendition of 'Spice Up Your Life'.

Ebi   So how'd you do?

Beat. **Bess** *digs out her change and counts.*

Bess   £4.20.

Ebi *stares.*

Bess   Don't look at me like that. Don't give me that, Ebi.

Ebi   £4.20? That's your contribution is it? That's what you're bringing in?

Bess   I had a bad day.

Ebi   A bad day? That's a travesty that is. How we going to get food in if you're bringing back £4 a day?

Bess   £4.20 and it was a one-off. We've got some saved.

Ebi   Can't be relying on that.

Bess   Well how did you do then? Mr High and Mighty.

Ebi   Better than you.

Bess   Go on.

Ebi   £9 flat.

Bess *sighs.*

Ebi   Told you.

Bess   Still working the same place?

Ebi   Same place, same time. People like a bit of routine, makes it easier for them to trust.

Bess   Makes it easier for them to ignore.

Ebi   That's always easy. It's no good walking around town hoping for a lucky find, Bess, thought you might know that by now.

Bess   Here we go.

Ebi   My spot isn't glitzy, it isn't that busy, but come 5 o'clock I get tow hours of solid traffic pouring out of them office blocks. And I knows every one of them. Hard to ignore a face you recognise. It's about building a relationship.

Bess   Until they get bored of you. Pass the same man every day with his hand out and they'll start thinkin' you might be taking the piss. Then we'll see how much you get.

Ebi   I prefer to put my faith in a little thing called human decency.

Bess   Get out with that bollocks.

Ebi   Done me alright today, hasn't it? You're the one with no money. I'm sitting pretty.

Bess   Oh yeh, Beverly Hills this.

Ebi   It's dry, it's safe.

Bess   Exactly, we found a spot where we can get out of the rain and no one's going to kick our heads in, and we think we've hit the bloody jackpot. But no, I mustn't complain, we've got a fire.

Ebi   I got some sandwiches too if you're hungry.

Bess (*sarcastically*)   Happy days.

Beat.

Bess   You seen Hannah?

Ebi *gestures behind him.*

Bess   Bloody hell, How long's she been like that?

Ebi   Well, I came back when it started raining and she was already off her head. Passed out not soon after.

Bess   So she's been there this whole time?

Ebi   Yeh.

Bess   Lucky you came back.

Ebi   Yeh.

Bess   She's getting worse.

Ebi   Yeh.

Bess *looks over.*

Bess   You're bringing all the chat today aren't you, Ebi?

Beat. She opens a knackered old tobacco tin and starts trying to piece together a fag. Realising she doesn't have enough she looks up.

Bess   Got a smoke?

Ebi   I don't –

Bess   You don't smoke, I forgot.

Ebi   You always forget. Got a soggy brain.

Bess   Piss off.

She looks around slowly, finally settling on **Hannah**. *She moves towards her and begins going through her pockets.*

Ebi   Come on, Bess.

Bess   Leave it, I couldn't pick any up in the rain, they were all wet.

Ebi   What makes you think she'll have any?

Bess   She's always got some baccy for that shit she smokes.

Ebi   That's low.

Bess (*of* **Hannah**)   No, this is low. Completely fucking useless she is.

Bess *eventually digs out a cigarette tin and marches back to the fire with a pre-rolled fag.*

Bess (*of the fag*)   Least she spent her day doing something.

Ebi   Sure that's safe? Don't want to go losing your head.

Bess *sniffs the cigarette suspiciously.*

Bess   Seems alright.

She puts it in her mouth and begins patting her pockets. Realising she has no lighter she returns to **Hannah**'s *pockets.* **Hannah** *has begun to stir.*

Hannah (*high pitched and grating, sleepy*)   Was' going' on?

Bess   Nothin' go back to sleep.

Hannah (*resisting pathetically*)   What you doing?

Bess   Where's your lighter?

Hannah   Don't have one.

Bess   Yes you do.

Ebi   That's not right, Bess.

Bess   Stay out of this. Come on, where is it?

She flips a groggy **Hannah** *onto her front and goes into a back pocket where she finds a lighter.* **Hannah** *is recovering/trying to wake up.*

Hannah   Fuckin' hell, I don't have nothing!

Bess   Liar.

She heads back to **Ebi**. **Hannah** *goes still again.*

Ebi   Not the nicest way to treat her.

Bess   Shut up.

Ebi   You watch now, she'll be screaming blue murder.

Bess   No, she'll be drifting back to cloud cuckoo land.

Hannah *sits bolt upright.*

Hannah   I've been robbed!

Ebi   Told you.

Hannah   Someone's been having my stuff!

Bess   Shut up.

Hannah   I rest my eyes for two seconds and you monsters start trawling through my pockets.

Ebi   Leave me out of it.

Hannah   What'd I do to deserve this?

Bess   You don't know what you're talking about, Han! All that stuff you smoke has been rotting your brain. I told you that before.

Hannah   Oh, leave me be, Bess. I'm getting my bearings aren't I? Don't have a go.

She slumps back down dramatically not fully aware of where she is.

Bess *sighs with exasperation.*

Ebi   There's a bottle in my tent. And give that back.

Bess *collects the lighter and case before heading off to* **Ebi**'s *tent. On the way she stops by* **Hannah** *and attempts to replace what she took in the inside pocket.* **Hannah**, *suspecting further thieving, starts to put up a ham-karate resistance which is more an annoyance to* **Bess** *than a genuine threat.*

Hannah   Back up or I'll chop ya!

Bess *keeps faffing. Eventually* **Hannah** *lands a light blow on* **Bess**'s *face/shoulder.* **Bess** *loses patience and flings the case and lighter at* **Hannah** *who slowly starts collecting them.* **Bess** *returns to the fire.*

Bess   Ah fuck this! You get it, Ebi, I'm not dealing with her.

Ebi *goes to get water from his tent. On the way back he gives it to* **Hannah**.

Ebi   Not that you deserve it.

Hannah   Thanks, Ebi. You're a saint you are, one of the good ones.

Ebi   You shouldn't be smoking so much.

Hannah   Why not? I bought it with my own money.

Bess   Did you fuck. You scammed it off Georgie cos he's got the hots for you.

Hannah   Didn't.

Bess   Did. Told me himself he gave it you. And it's the group's money, how many more times? We all pitch in, we all take out.

Hannah   Go easy, Bess.

Bess   You're puffing away whatever brain you got left.

Ebi   Yeh, it was a good job I came back when I did or you'd have been passed out on the floor. Anyone could have come in here, taken our stuff.

Bess   We're out there getting money and food for you, and you're in here leaving the whole place free to whoever wants it.

Hannah   You got food?

Bess   Jesus Christ.

Ebi   Got some sandwiches here. If you can make it.

Hannah *gives an overly dramatic account of not being able to get up*.

Bess   Unbelievable. Look at yourself.

Hannah   Don't be like that.

Bess   You should be embarrassed.

Hannah   Come on, Bess. We've all got our little troubles.

Ebi   Oh, don't start, Hannah.

Bess   What's that supposed to mean?

Hannah   What? We've all got our problems don't we?

Ebi   Don't start.

Hannah (*carrying on*)   I like a puff, you like a drink, Ebi . . . well Ebi's wife used to beat him didn't she? So I reckon he just enjoys not being found.

Ebi   Oi!

Bess   What do you mean, I enjoy a drink? How dare you.

Ebi   Don't bite, Bess. She's just being a little shit.

Bess   Stay out of this. What did you mean?

Ebi   Don't bite.

Hannah   You know what I mean. You're a fiend for it.

Bess   For what?

Hannah   Come on. We're all friends here.

Bess   What? So sometimes, on occasion, I'll choose to get a bit merry, that does not make me a fiend –

Hannah   Ha! A bit merry? Hear that, Ebi?

Ebi   She does have a point, Bess.

Hannah   Remember that time you hit the jackpot and found a wallet with £100 in it? It was gone in a day.

Bess   Wasn't.

Ebi   Less than that I think.

Bess   It was not!

Hannah   It bloody was. You ended up getting so pissed you wet yourself –

Ebi   And then tried to go dancing.

Hannah (*laughing*)   Yes she did! She did try to go fucking dancing. Stood outside of Tiger Tiger with a pair of soaking trousers, telling them all to make way for the funk.

They fall about laughing.

Bess   It weren't like that, it weren't like that.

Hannah   That bouncer sent you flying.

Ebi   You hit the ground so hard you got hiccups.

Bess   Still went dancing though didn't I?

Ebi   That poor girl, bet she never celebrates her birthday with a house party again.

Bess   Oh, they were loving it. Best night they ever had.

Ebi   They called the police.

Bess   Yeh, only cos the party got out of hand.

Hannah   The party? You robbed some kid in the loo, started doing lines off the kitchen counter and touched up the birthday girl. The party had nothing to do with it.

Bess   Piss off.

Ebi   Hear that, Hannah? Piss off!

They laugh. The chuckles die down. **Bess** *is fuming.*

Ebi   Don't sulk Bess.

Hannah   Yeh, just saying we've all got our own little troubles, doesn't everyone? I'm not perfect.

Bess   Far from it.

Hannah   Exactly. So how about a hand up?

They go and collect **Hannah**, *who is still pretty weak, and bring her to the fire. They support her.*

Hannah   Thanks, Bess. You too, Ebi. Really appreciate that. And I'm sorry about taking a nap when I was supposed to be watching the stuff, won't happen again.

Bess   Heard that before.

Hannah   No, I'll do us good tomorrow, when do I ever come back with less than £15? I'll bring us all some hot food, it'll be great. Hey, we should pack up for a night, maybe see if there's a few free beds in any of the shelters.

Ebi *snorts with laughter.*

Hannah   Why not?

Bess   I'm sure that'll work. Three beds, ready and waiting.

Ebi   Like Goldilocks.

Bess   Hot food. Helpful staff.

Ebi   Nice, sociable neighbours.

Bess   Here, Ebi, what happened to you last time you managed to get a bed?

Ebi   All my stuff got nicked and I left with a headful of lice.

Bess   Any idea how hard it is to shift head lice when you're sleeping rough?

Ebi   Besides, you can't go two hours without a puff of spice so you got no chance.

Hannah   I can.

Bess   Bollocks. Second you light up in the bogs, or break curfew to sneak one outside, you're gone.

Ebi   And you got lice.

Bess   We'd have to shave you.

Ebi   From here to Highgate you'd be known as The Baldy Beggar.

Bess Don't reckon Georgie would be so generous after that, now would he?

Hannah Fuckin' hell.

Ebi Them hostels might sound nice but they'll set you back a long way, trust me on that.

Hannah Jesus, that's depressing.

Bess Listen, you're good here, you're doing well. I've got you registered at the council and you're on the housing list. All you got to do is wait here with us.

Hannah You said, they said it could be years.

Ebi Well sure, worst-case scenario. But a young thing like yourself? No, no, they got an interest in helping you. Any day now I reckon. Any day. You'll be warm, dry and safe on your feet.

Beat.

Hannah What're you lot going to do then?

Bess Ah, we'll work something out. Been out here long enough to know our way around, ain't that right, Ebi?

Ebi Right enough.

Beat.

Hannah Thanks, guys. I'd be fucked without you. Totally fucked.

Ebi Ah, let's have none of that. Just lay off the bloody spice is all.

Hannah Yeh. Yeh course. I'll be better tomorrow, I'll rake it in.

Ebi Well, anything'll be better than today.

Bess Ebi.

Hannah What happened today?

Bess   Nothing.

Hannah   Someone been giving you trouble?

Ebi   No one's been giving her anything, that's the problem.

Bess   You are pushing me, Ebi.

Hannah   What, money?

Bess   It's nothing.

Hannah   How much did you get?

Pause. Just as **Bess** *is about to speak* **Ebi** *jumps in. Throughout the following exchange* **Caz** *enters behind the group. She has a black eye, is wet and looks around furtively before approaching.*

Ebi   £4.00

Bess   £4.20.

Hannah   £4?

Bess   20! Jesus Christ.

Hannah   Oh, Bess.

Bess   Look, fuck off the both of you. It's easy for you lookin' like Bambi. People fling it at you.

Hannah   How'd you do?

Ebi   £9.

Hannah   Hey, that's not bad.

Ebi   Slow day as well.

Bess   Slow day for me too.

Ebi   We noticed.

Bess   It's different, you got a spot.

Hannah   I don't have a spot.

Ebi   She doesn't have a spot.

Bess   I swear to God, Ebi, one more word, just one more – !

Caz   Sorry to interrupt.

Big reaction. **Bess** *jumps,* **Ebi** *spins,* **Hannah***, unsupported, hits the deck.*

Ebi   Jesus!

Hannah   Oh!

Bess   Who the fuck are you?!

Caz   Well, that's charming that is.

Bess   Quick, put out the fire.

Ebi   No, no! We won't get it started again.

Bess   It might attract more people.

Caz   Don't worry, I'm on my own.

Bess *rounds on* **Caz***.*

Bess   I'll worry if I want to. Answer the question.

Caz   Which was?

Ebi/Hannah   Who the fuck are you?

Caz   This is some reception. I come up out of the rain, looking for a little bit of warmth and all I get is 'who are you'? Who'd you think I am? The Queen?

Hannah   What's your name?

Caz   What's your name?

Bess   You first.

Caz   Why me?

Ebi   Cos we say so.

Beat.

Caz   Caz.

Ebi   We don't know any Caz's.

Caz   Now you do.

Bess   No. We don't know anyone called Caz and we know everyone round here. Which means you're not from round here.

Hannah   So where you from?

Caz   Here and there.

Bess   Here and there?

Caz   Yeh. All over.

Bess   Never heard of it.

Ebi   Where have you just come from?

Caz   What's it to you, baldy?

Pause. Stand-off.

Caz   If I told you I was born in Portsmouth would you let me near that fire?

Bess   Didn't ask where you were born, I asked where you've come from.

Beat.

Caz   Just west of London.

Bess   Right. Ealing like?

Caz   Bit further than that.

Bess   Oh I see. Staines, by any chance?

Caz   Do you know it was? That's some good guessing.

Bess   Yeh. There's a big prison in Staines.

Caz   Indeed there is. Very big. Thought to myself 'that's one big prison', right as I walked past it.

Hannah   Or walked out of it.

Caz What was that?

Hannah Or did you walk out of it?

Caz That's a rude thing to say. Big accusation from such a young lady.

Ebi You're not so old yourself. You should be in a shelter.

Caz Yeh, but we both know it's not that simple.

Bess So you thought you'd try your luck with us?

Beat.

Caz Look, we've got off on the wrong foot. I'm new here, you got me, and I need somewhere to be.

Bess Find your own spot.

Caz You know what happens to girls on their own.

Hannah Bess?

Bess Not my problem.

Hannah Bess!

Bess What?

Hannah Let her stay.

Bess (*keeping her eyes fixed on* **Caz**)   I don't trust her.

Ebi Sounds like she needs help.

Bess She can help herself.

Hannah Your first night out here you got filled in by some lads who ended up pissing on you.

Bess Oi!

Caz (*cutting in*)   Do you like magic?

Ebi What?

Hannah Yes.

Bess   Shut up.

Caz   How's about I do some magic? Try and calm things down a bit?

Bess   What the fuck are you on?

Caz   I know she wants to see a trick, written all over her face. Tell you what, if you can tell me how I do it I'm gone, otherwise you let me kip here for one night.

Beat.

Go on, try me. Bet you can't work it out.

Beat.

Bess   Fine.

Caz (*clapping her hands*)   Right you are. All I need's a few moments by that fire and I'm good to go.

She moves to the centre of the group around the fire and starts warming herself.

Hannah   What sort of magic is it?

Ebi   The sort where you should keep your hands in your pockets.

Bess   Exactly.

Caz   You are suspicious. Someone must've really done a number on you lot.

Hannah   So what sort of magic?

Caz *produces a deck of cards and starts shuffling expertly over the fire.*

Caz   Oh, you'll find out. Now . . . Bess.

She holds out the deck. **Bess** *is taken aback.*

Bess   How you'd know that?

Caz   Excuse me?

Bess   How'd you know my name?

Ebi   Hannah said it two seconds ago.

Bess   Oh yeh.

Calm returns.

Caz   All ok? Right, Bess, cut the deck for me.

Bess *does so.*

Caz   Good. Now, Ebi wasn't it? Check my sleeves, make sure I've got nothing inside of them.

Ebi *does so.*

Caz   Good. Well, let's get started then. Young lady.

Hannah   Hannah.

Beat.

Caz   Hannah, pick a card.

She fans them out in front of **Hannah** *who looks around.*

Ebi   Go on.

Hannah *does.*

Caz   Now don't show it to me, but you lot can have a look. Right, now, you got it in your head?

Hannah *nods.*

Caz   Not going to go slipping out of there is it?

Hannah *shakes her head.*

Caz   Good, ok. Put it back in. Ebi, give them a good old shuffle for me.

Ebi *shuffles them, hands them back.*

Caz   Ok, now.

She fixes **Hannah** *with a stare. Throughout this fast exchange she's rifling through the cards.*

Caz   How old are you, Hannah?

Hannah   Nineteen.

Caz   And how long have you been out here?

Hannah   Just a few months.

Caz   And where are you from?

Hannah   Kent.

Caz   Where?

Hannah   Buryford.

Caz   Kicked out, moved out?

Hannah   Kicked out.

Caz   Trouble at home?

Hannah   Yeh.

Caz   Dad?

Hannah   Step-dad.

Caz   Neglectful?

Hannah   Yeh.

Caz   Abusive?

Hannah   Yep.

Caz (*quickly*)   Step-daddy took a shine to you soon as he moved in, Mum never cared that much in the first place so didn't do too much about it, eventually started getting jealous, kicked you out, so thought you'd try your luck in London where the streets are paved with gold?

Hannah   Yeh.

Caz *holds up the three of clubs.*

Caz   Is this your card?

Ebi   Oh!

Hannah   Fuckin' hell.

Caz   I'll take that as a yes.

Hannah   How'd you do that?

Caz   Told you I was magic, didn't I?

Hannah   She did, she did say that.

Bess   But how'd you really do it?

Caz   I'm really magic.

Bess   Bollocks.

Hannah   Then how'd she guess my card?

Caz   Can't argue with that.

Ebi   It was a trick.

Bess   Exactly, it was a trick.

Caz   Call it what you like.

Bess   Card was probably still warm from where you'd been touching it. Just needed time to find the warm one.

Caz   Warm? On a night like this? Think these things are made from asbestos?

Bess   Well I'm just sayin' it weren't magic.

Hannah   Seemed like magic to me. You're a class act you are.

Caz   Why, thank you. Anyone know how I did it?

Pause.

No? Well, we did agree that means I can stay here tonight.

Pause. No movement.

Please?

Pause.

(*Seriously.*) Please.

Hannah *raises her hand dramatically.*

Bess   What you doing?

Hannah   I'm voting. I'm sayin' she can stay.

Caz   Thank you.

Bess   It's not that simple.

Hannah   Course it is. She can do magic.

Ebi   So can Derren Brown. Doesn't mean I want him sharing my tent.

Caz   No need for sharing. Got me a mat and bag in here.

Long pause.

Bess   Cost you.

Caz   What?

Bess   You heard.

Hannah   Bess!

Caz   Cost me what?

Bess   Money. We found this place, we got all the tents and that, the drum, the wood. It's our spot, so you gotta pay.

Hannah   I didn't have to pay.

Bess   That was different.

Hannah   Don't take it out on her just cos you had a bad day.

Bess   Shut up.

Caz   How bad a day was it, Bess?

Bess   None of you, business.

Pause. Stand-off.

Caz   Well, I can't pay you any money.

Bess   Then you can't kip by our fire.

Caz   But in place of money I can offer you this.

From her backpack she pulls a quart of Sainsbury's own brand whiskey.

Silence.

I reckon this is better than a few quid, way you're looking at it, Bess. Split it four ways, sit around this fire and we can all be friends. How's that?

Ebi   Where'd you get that?

Caz   Some kind soul in Golders Green thought I might have need of it.

Ebi   Means she stole it. She stole it.

Hannah   So?

Ebi   So, we don't want someone here who's got the police looking for them. They'll smash this place right up.

Caz   I got this fair and square, nothing to worry about. Come on, not going to turn down a drink are you?

Beat.

Bess   You can sleep over there (*She gestures to downstage left*). Gimme.

Caz *hands over the bottle. The others rush into their tents and exit with cups before* **Bess**, *who's already started swigging, can get through too much. They form a semi-circle of* **Hannah**, **Bess**, **Ebi** *and* **Caz**.

Ebi   Hey, hey! Give me some of that!

Bess *reluctantly pours into the cups. When they are all full she returns to her spot and leaves the bottle by her leg.*

Caz   Why don't you hang onto that, Bess?

Bess   Think I will.

They all drink. Beat.

Caz   So, what brings you all here?

Bess   Ah, just wanted to lose some weight.

Caz (*playing along*)   Really?

Bess   Yeh, Hannah wanted to get out more and Ebi just loves the lifestyle. Any more stupid questions?

Ebi *laughs.*

Caz   Well I didn't mean that. I meant, why are you lot here?

Ebi   Eh?

Caz   Well, there's nicer places to be than tucked away under the arches.

Hannah   Like where?

Caz   For starters you'd be warmer in a station.

Bess   Off you go then.

Caz   Jesus, I'm just saying, it's a bit of an odd arrangement, isn't it? This. Two older faces taking care of some young'un. Not something you see everyday.

Ebi   We all got to stick together.

Caz (*of* **Bess**)   She don't strike me as the most inclusive type. (*Beat.*) You should try a different spot, lots of places with better pickings, more hostels. You two could even try for a women's shelter.

Bess   We're safer here. Hidden.

Caz   What if someone finds you?

Bess   Someone like you?

Caz   Maybe. Maybe someone who wouldn't mind stumbling into a group of girls. (*To* **Ebi**.) No offence. You know what happens then. Way I heard it, Bess, you know all about it.

Bess   Judging by your eye you know all about it too. Kiss with a fist was it?

Caz   Something like that.

Beat.

Why not try a squat? Better than this.

Hannah   Can't.

Caz   And why's that, my love?

Hannah   Get a criminal record.

Caz   We've all got records.

Hannah   Not me. And I'm waiting on a house.

Caz   Is that a fact?

Hannah   Yeh.

Caz   When's it due?

Hannah   Any day now –

Bess   Couple of years.

Hannah   You said –

Bess   I know what I said.

Beat.

Caz   Couple of years, right. And what happens to you two when she lands the penthouse?

Ebi   We'll figure something out.

Bess *gets up to top* **Hannah**, **Ebi** *and herself up, finishing the bottle.*

Caz   I see. Very decent of you, very unusual. Do top yourself up.

By the time **Bess** *gets to* **Caz** *the bottle is empty.*

Bess   Ah, will you look at that.

Caz   Not to worry. These things happen.

Bess *takes the bottle back to her spot.*

Ebi   If you like squats so much, why don't you try one?

Caz   Maybe I will. Know any round here?

Ebi   No.

Caz   Ah, that's alright. I usually end up on my feet.

Bess   Says the tramp.

Caz   Well, no point thinking about tomorrow tonight, is there?

Hannah   Exactly, specially when we've got a magician in the mix.

Caz (*waves her off modestly*)   Ah, stop.

Hannah   Go on. Do another for us.

Caz   I couldn't possibly.

Bess   What a shame.

Hannah   Go on!

Ebi   Yeh, I wouldn't mind seeing another.

Beat.

Caz   Well, if you insist.

Excitement builds. She stands.

If you'd step over here, young lady.

Hannah *races over.*

Caz   Just like that, very good. Now, I want you to think of a letter –

Bess   Barking up the wrong tree mate, she can't read!

Hannah   Shut up, Bess. I can.

Ebi   No you can't.

Hannah   Leave it, Ebi! I can think of a fucking letter!

Caz (*whistling*)   Over here.

Hannah *turns back to* **Caz**.

Caz   You got one?

Hannah   Yeh.

Caz   Right, keep focusing on it. Don't mind them, just focus on me.

Hannah *nods*.

Caz   Good, now.

She closes her eyes and takes both of **Hannah***'s hands, palms up, in hers, thumbs resting on* **Hannah***'s pulse. She pulls a face of struggling concentration. As the tension reaches its peak she breaks.*

Caz   No, sorry can't be doing it.

Bess *laughs harshly.*

Hannah   What?

Caz   It's not working.

Bess   No good without them cards are you? About as magic as my arse.

Caz *is straining as if trying to sort out her head.*

Caz   It's not the cards, it's, it's something else, something in my . . . I know what it is! I need a drink, a little top-up.

Bess   Bottle's empty.

Caz   Is it?

Bess   Yep, just drank the last of it.

Beat.

Caz   You sure about that?

Bess *raises the bottle. It's full. The others turn in awe.*

Bess   Fuck me.

Caz   Told you.

Lights snap down.

Scene Two

The camp, two weeks later. **Bess** *and* **Ebi** *are waiting for the others to return. The mood is tense and frustrated.* **Ebi** *sits while* **Bess** *paces around the camp.*

Bess   Where is she?

Ebi   Don't know.

Bess   You been out all day, how can you not know?

Ebi   Cos I didn't see her. We don't usually see each other when we're out. Why are you so worried?

Bess   Because you only brought back £6.

Ebi   It was busy. Lots of other people.

Bess   It's always busy, you got to be more forceful. If someone else starts begging near your spot you got to show them the boot, move them on.

Ebi   Oh, is that how you do it?

Bess   What does that mean?

Ebi   Been a while since you brought back more'n £6.

Bess   What, so people can be cold hearted when you look a bit older, that's on me is it?

He doesn't respond.

Bess   This is your fault anyway.

Ebi   How's that?

Bess   You let that snake in.

Ebi   Eh?

Bess   I said one night, that was the deal, but two weeks later, she's still here.

Ebi   How's that my fault? Besides, she brings in a lot. And we could use it.

Bess   I don't trust her. Hannah would never be this late before.

Ebi   You're paranoid.

Bess   How come someone like that's homeless anyway?

Ebi   You what?

Bess   Well, she's smart, got a bit of something, what's she doing here?

Ebi   I'm an electrician, what am I doing here? What's anyone doing here? It's bad luck, that's all.

Bess   What if her and Hannah take off? Decide they're better off on their own?

Ebi   She wouldn't do that.

Bess   Why not?

Ebi   We helped her, took her in. She owes us.

Bess   When's that ever counted for anything? So what if she owes us? No bloody rules out here. She'd roll on you same as you'd roll on me.

Ebi   I'd never.

Bess   I'd roll on you.

Beat.

Ebi   Don't talk like that. We're going to stick it out, she'll get the house and before you know it we'll be warm, dry and kipping on the sofa. Best idea you ever had.

Bess   Yeh. Sure.

Beat.

Ebi   You alright?

Beat. She gestures to the world around her with an incredulous face.

Bess   Yeh, couldn't be better.

We hear **Caz** *and* **Hannah** *from offstage.*

Ebi   Here we go.

Enter **Caz** *and* **Hannah**. *They're enjoying themselves, pleased with how the day has gone. Each holds a plastic bag.*

Hannah   Alright you two?

Ebi   Alright?

Caz   Alright, Ebi?

Ebi   Alright.

Bess   About time.

Caz   Told you.

Bess   Told her what?

Hannah   Caz said you'd be mardy.

Bess   Did she really? Where you been?

Hannah   Out.

Bess   Out?

Hannah   Yeh.

Bess   What good is 'out' to us? We're supposed to be a bloody group.

Hannah   Chill out.

Bess   You're not acting like part of a group.

Caz   Guess you won't be wanting these chips then?

Beat.

Ebi   Are they warm?

Caz   Scalding.

Ebi *runs over and grabs a box. He rams them into his mouth contentedly.*

Ebi   Oh my God, that's beautiful that is. Didn't get a bite all day.

Hannah   Thought you'd be happy.

Caz   Got everyone a few cans as well. Thought you might like that, Bess.

They drop chips and cans where **Bess** *is sitting. After initial reluctance she starts eating.*

Ebi   So, how'd you do?

Hannah   £30.

Ebi   Not bad.

Hannah   Each.

Bess   You what?

Hannah   Well, I made £20, Caz made £40.

Ebi   Fuck me, that's impressive.

Caz   Easy when you got something they wanna see.

She flourishes the cards.

Ebi   Unbelievable, £60. Where were you?

Caz   High street.

Bess   Tough spot.

Hannah   Not for her it's not.

Caz   God these chips are good. Tell you what, it's not an easy life, but on a day like today, no rain, money coming in, chips, can, ain't half bad.

Hannah   Yeh, it felt really good today. I was enjoying myself.

Ebi Jesus, I can't remember the last time I felt like that.

Caz Well, you should come out with us, Ebi. We had a laugh, didn't we Han?

Hannah Yeh.

Ebi Oh, I don't know.

Caz Give it a try, Ebi. Hang around with a grumpy twat like Bess too long and you'll end up on the Archway bridge.

Hannah *barks a laugh.*

Bess Look at you, all pleased with yourself just cos you can do a card trick.

Ebi D'you reckon you could teach me?

Caz Maybe, maybe not.

Bess Bollocks. Course she could, she could teach anyone. And if you had a good bone in your body you'd be teaching us, the people who let you stay here, so we could all get some cash out of it too.

Caz Takes a special kind of person.

Bess Does it fuck. It takes a rigged deck.

Caz Is that so?

Bess Course. If you know the pack anyone can do it.

Hannah What about the bottle? That weren't rigged.

Bess Sleight of hand. She must have moved it before and I didn't notice.

Caz Makes you pretty thick doesn't it, Bess?

Bess No one ever notices they're getting played, that's how it happens. You'd do well to remember that, Hannah.

Caz I agree. She would.

Beat.

She takes out all the money and starts counting. **Hannah** *opens a tobacco tin and starts rolling a spliff.*

Caz   Right, we got £20 from Hannah, 40 from me makes 60, what'd you get, Ebi?

Ebi (*sheepishly handing over his money*)   £6.

Caz   Tell us another.

Hannah   £6?

Ebi   It was busy.

Caz   I'm well aware.

Ebi   It was busy, just leave it.

Beat.

Caz   Right, well, our 60 plus a last-minute surge in capital takes us to 66 minus £9 for chips and cans leaves us with £57, that's 50 and 7. Not bad.

Ebi   Not bad at all, that'll keep us good for a while.

Hannah (*to* **Ebi**)   No thanks to you.

Bess   Watch it.

Caz   Wonder what it'll be like tomorrow. My day off isn't it? Means we'll have to rely on you two. Bit scary that.

Bess   We'll be fine. It's you I'm worried about, they'll get used to your card tricks eventually and then you'll have to find something new.

Caz   I got plenty of tricks.

Hannah (*excited*)   Go on then.

Ebi   Yeh, go on. Show us one.

Bess (*sarcastically*)   Yeh, Caz, show us one.

Beat.

Caz   Alright.

She stands, as does **Hannah***, expecting the trick to involve her.* **Ebi**
stands but as a spectator. **Caz** *withdraws her cards.*

Caz   Come here, Ebi.

Ebi   Oh, right.

He moves forward.

Caz   Now, I want you to pick three cards from this deck –

Bess   I got an idea. Why don't you try something without
the cards?

Beat.

Caz   Fine. (*She pockets the deck.*) This time I want you to
think of a number between one and ten –

Bess   Grey elephants in Denmark.

Ebi   Shut up, Bess, it's my turn.

Beat.

Caz   Good lad. Now, think of a number between one and
ten. Got it?

Ebi *nods.*

Caz   Good, now, I'm going to shut my eyes and I want you
to whisper it to Hannah over there ok?

Ebi *nods.* **Caz** *turns away and covers her eyes,* **Ebi** *whispers to*
Hannah*.*

Caz   All done? Good. Come here, closer, closer, right in
front of me, that's it. Now look at me.

Ebi *smiles awkwardly and looks around.*

Caz   Don't look at her, look at me. Keep looking.

Pause. The stare continues.

Caz   Seven.

Hannah   Oh. My. God.

Ebi   That's crazy.

Caz   Was seven your number?

Ebi   You know it was.

Caz   Hannah?

Hannah   It was. Oh my God, it was.

Caz   There you are, Bess, new trick.

Ebi   Jesus Christ, that is amazing.

Hannah   You're incredible.

Ebi   How is that possible? (*To* **Hannah**.) I mean, how is that even possible?

Hannah (*reaching an insane level of highness and excitement*)   I don't believe this, you're just, I mean I – I wouldn't even – I can't – If I had to – Fucking hell.

She passes out dramatically.

Caz   Well that's never happened before.

Bess   Don't flatter yourself. It's that spice stuff, knocks her clean out sometimes.

Ebi   How'd you do that?

Caz   Magic.

Ebi   Who taught you?

Caz   That'd be telling.

Ebi   Go on.

Caz *withdraws the cards and shuffles while she talks.*

Caz   Alright. It was this guy called Charlie. When I first started sleeping out I was doing the hostel circuit, like everyone, all the waiting and that, and then one night there he was next to me in the queue. Weird bloke, really quiet and paranoid to fuck but what he could do was magic.

Amazing stuff. So I managed to convince Charlie that
spending four hours a day queuing for a bed and having
people search your room and all the fights and the smack-
heads just wasn't worth it, and that we could spend that time
earning good money doing magic tricks in town.

Ebi   And?

Caz   We did. It was a bit quiet while he taught me but after
a while my natural flair took over and we had an alright time
of it.

Ebi   So where is he now?

Caz   Well, I found some fella who got me off the street for a
couple of years and he didn't like what I had with Charlie so,
seeing as this bloke had a bed, we went our separate ways.
Think he tried it for a bit but he wasn't that good at being on
his own. By the time I was back out here, no one had seen
him for months.

Ebi   What happened to him?

Caz   Nothing good I reckon.

Bess (*breaking the moment*)   Ah, sure he's fine.

Caz   You should find him, Bess. Ask him for tips.

Pause.

Bess (*of* **Hannah**)   You two seem to be getting along.

Caz   Yeh.

Beat.

Bess   Thought you were only staying a night.

Caz   So did I.

Bess   It's been over two weeks now. Thought you'd have
moved on.

Caz   Thing is, I like it here.

Bess Do you?

Caz I do. Like you lot, like the group, like all of it. Only thing I cannot understand is why you keep living under these arches.

Ebi It's safe.

Caz Not really.

Ebi Sure it is. We're 30 metres from the main road that way and the only thing down there is a gated car park, safe as can be.

Bess Where would you go?

Caz Told you before, I'd get in a squat. You got shelter in a squat, you can rig up the electrics, bit of heat, bit of cooking. You got rights as well.

Bess I stayed in one for a while. Horrible people there. I know people who've died in squats.

Caz And I know people who've been kicked to death in their sleeping bags.

Bess Well, clearly we disagree on what's best for the group, so why don't you just go?

Caz What? Pretty young thing like me, walk straight into someone else's squat? Not on your life, Bess, said it yourself, horrible people there. No, no. I need a group, a team, people who'll watch out for each other. A little bit like you lot.

Bess You stay away from my group.

Caz *smiles. Beat.*

Caz Your group is it? How'd you feel about that, Ebi?

Ebi Well, I, at the end of the day, when all's said and done – y'know.

Caz Well said. (*Beat.*) You just don't want her meeting new people.

Bess   Why would we care?

Caz   Don't want that £20 a day going to anyone else.

Bess   You might think like that, but it's fair, we do lots of stuff for her. Ain't that right, Ebi?

Ebi   Oh, right enough. She wouldn't want a squat.

Caz   Seemed quite taken with the idea today.

Bess   Not when you're risking a record, hard to get a council house with that.

Caz   Oh I see. You're just looking after her interests with the council.

Bess   That's right.

Caz   Funny thing she told me today, she said that you, Bess, were sorting out her application for emergency accommodation.

Bess   Well, she's got to be registered as homeless first.

Caz   And you're sorting that?

Bess   Yes.

Caz   Both of you?

Ebi   No, no. I don't understand it.

Caz   But you do?

Bess   Some, yeh. Poor girl can barely read, I'm trying to help her. When she's not passed out, she's talking to the fucking pixies, if she walks into the council like that they'll send her right back, with the same bloody pamphlets they've been giving out for years. Might as well be in Italian for all the good they'll do her.

Ebi   She's right.

Bess   So yes, I'm helping her get sorted. Look, when we met her she was walking down Camden High Street in the middle of the night asking for places to stay. How do you think that was going to end? So I helped.

Caz And she's been with you two ever since?

Ebi 'Bout seven months now.

Caz That's odd. Should only take a few weeks to get registered.

Bess Welcome to London. There's twice as many of us here as there was six years ago. Hostels shutting down all over the place. Two in Westminster, the one in Parker Street, Dean Street. There's no room, and there's too many of us.

Ebi Too many of them. Those bloody illegals come here, looking for the jobs we already lost and end up taking our beds in the shelters. It's disgusting.

Bess Too right.

Ebi Always banging on about restrictions and less people coming over. But every time I'm waiting in line for something there's five more Wladimirs pushing in front of me.

Caz Won't argue with you on that. But what happens when she finally gets the house? You two going to pack her off with a kiss and then be on your way?

Bess We'll figure something out.

Caz Seven months to get registered? I think you've figured something out already.

Ebi What you talking about?

Bess She's talking about nothing, don't you listen to a word she says. And I've figured out how you do your shitty little trick.

Caz Oh yeh?

Bess Yeh. You made Ebi tell his number to Hannah.

Caz So?

Bess So just like that Charlie bloke all you've done is gone and got yourself an assistant.

She points to the passed out **Hannah** *lying centre stage.*

Ebi   She didn't say anything.

Bess   Not with her voice. Probably got a little system worked out, all that time they spent together today. They played you rotten, Ebi.

Caz   Why don't you have a go, Bess? You can tell your number to Ebi, or do you reckon we've got a system going too?

Ebi   We don't.

Bess   You might do, can't be sure.

Ebi   Oi.

Caz   Guess you'll never know then.

Beat. Stand-off.

Bess   Gimme that deck of yours.

Caz   What?

Bess   You heard. Gimme your cards.

Beat. **Caz** *hesitates.*

Bess   Go on. If it's just a normal deck . . .

Beat.

Bess   See, Ebi, told you she's hiding something –

Caz *hands it over.* **Bess** *takes it and strides away, rifling through the cards, chuckling to herself.*

Bess   Right, I've picked a card. What is it?

Caz   You'll lie.

Bess   Won't.

Caz   Course you will. You're lying all the time.

Beat.

Put it on the floor, face down, that way you can be sure no one else has seen it.

Beat. The tension mounts. **Bess** *and* **Caz** *are now facing each other across the downstage.* **Hannah,** *passed out, and* **Ebi** *sit together upstage centre.*

Bess *extracts her card and places it ceremoniously about 3 foot in front of* **Ebi,** *then returns to centre stage. Throughout this exchange* **Caz** *draws closer.*

Caz   Good. You focusing on that card?

Bess   Yep.

Caz   Got it right there in your mind?

Bess   Yep.

Caz   Ok. (*Beat.*) Look at me.

Bess   I am looking at you.

Beat.

Caz   Keep going.

Beat.

That's it, keep looking.

Beat. **Bess** *begins to frown.* **Caz** *cocks her head.*

Caz   Oh, Bess. You shouldn't make it that easy.

She breaks the stare and strides away before turning with a flourish and announcing:

The ace of spades.

Bess *stays frozen. Minor beat, as* **Ebi** *looks at the card, then leaps on it.*

Ebi   Oh my fucking God!

Caz   Am I right?

Ebi   It's the ace! Caz, it's the fucking ace.

Caz   Magic enough for you?

Ebi   Jesus Christ, Caz, you are – that's –

Lost for words, he begins to simply applaud. **Caz** *smugly sits down downstage left.* **Bess** *paces furiously upstage right.*

Bess   Stop that.

Ebi   You've got to give it to her, Bess, that was fucking incredible.

Bess   Stop it!

Silence.

How did you do that?

Caz   Magic.

Ebi   You know what? I'm starting to think you might be.

Bess   There's no such thing as magic, you twat!

Caz   Every time you say that a fairy dies.

Bess   Shut up! How did you do that?

Caz   Magic.

Bess *is getting closer, just the fire between them.* **Ebi** *is beginning to pick up on the tension.*

Bess   Fuck you. What number am I thinking of now?

Caz   Show's over.

Bess   What number?

Caz   Show's over.

Ebi   Bess.

Bess   No it's not. It's my camp, I'll say when it's over. What number am I thinking of now, you freak?

Ebi   Bess!

Caz   You're not thinking of a number.

Bess   Oh no?

Caz   No. You're wondering will I fight back if you hit me.

Bess   Well?

Caz *leaps up, ready to fight.* **Ebi** *joins.*

Caz   Come find out!

Bess   Finally.

Ebi   Jesus Christ, calm down!

Caz   I've been in this life since I was sixteen, what can you possibly to do me?

The tents around begin to glow from within, like a charge is pouring out of her. **Hannah** *begins to come round.*

Caz (*deeply, hard*)   I'm built like stone, girl. Course I fight back. Come at me I'll rip your fucking head off.

Bess   Let's see, then!

Hannah   What's goin' on?

The moment dissipates, a lingering tension remains. **Caz** *is the first to react.*

Caz   Your mum's been trying to guess how I do my tricks.

Hannah (*stretching out, yawning*)   Obvious innit? She's magic.

Caz *opens her arms to receive the compliment, staring at* **Bess**.

Caz   See?

Hannah   Like Jesus you are, come here to save us. Money, food, drink, you can make it happen just like that. (*She clicks and passes out again.*)

Caz   Hear that? Like Jesus.

Lights.

Scene Three

The camp. **Bess**, **Hannah** *and* **Ebi** *are about to start work. In the middle of the camp are three separate heaps, one of jackets one of trousers, one of shoes. In front of the heaps of clothes are basic sewing implements (needle and a few spools of thread); in front of the shoes is a roll of silver duct tape.* **Hannah** *is rolling a fag as* **Bess** *commands the space.*

As the lights come up there is a snap of energy.

Bess   Right! There's tape over there for the shoes, jackets in the middle and trousers over there. Careful with the needles, they only gave us a couple.

Ebi   I'll tape. Sewed last time.

Bess   Fine, Hannah?

Hannah   Jackets.

Bess   And I'll take trousers. Let's get shifting before the light goes.

They all walk to their places and start work.

Ebi (*of* **Hannah**'s *cigarette*)   Eh, eh! Make sure you're not ashing over anything. I don't want little holes in my trousers.

Hannah   Oh, Ebi, a little hole's all you need.

Bess *laughs.*

Bess   It's true.

Ebi   Yeh, funny. And that better just be a fag. It's fiddly work this.

Hannah *blows smoke his way.* **Ebi** *sniffs.*

Ebi   Fine.

Hannah   Where'd you get the stuff from?

Bess   I went up to St Matthew's off Goodge Street. They tend to come through for me once a year when they're feeling generous.

Hannah   Come through with what?

Bess   All sorts. Shoes, bags.

Ebi   You got that tent off 'em, didn't you?

Bess   Yeh, that were a couple of years back now.

Hannah   I didn't know you went to church.

Bess   I don't.

Ebi   She just speaks the language. Her dad was a priest –

Bess   No he wasn't.

Hannah   You're dad was a priest? Bloody hell, Bess.

Bess   He wasn't. He was just very religious, that's all. Used to go to church a lot, but he wasn't the one talking.

Hannah   Well, I was gonna say . . .

Beat.

Bess   Gonna say what?

Hannah   Well, just that if you're old man was a priest you probably wouldn't be here cos – cos he'd have had like a direct connection to – y'know, to the big man.

Beat. **Ebi** *and* **Bess** *laugh.*

Ebi   Right.

Hannah   What? What's so funny about that?

Bess   No, no it's just – I never thought of it that way.

Hannah   Well you should've.

Bess   Reckon that's why Sal's always lugging a Bible around? Trying to pray her way into a shelter?

Hannah   Makes sense though, doesn't it? You ever met a priest's kid out here?

Ebi   Never met a banker's kid out here neither but I don't think it's 'cos they're in touch with the divine.

Hannah   You laugh, Ebi, you laugh . . .

They settle down to work again.

Beat.

Ebi (*trying to be casual*)   Anyone seen Caz?

Hannah   Not since she left this morning.

Bess   Never know, today might be the day.

Hannah   When what?

Bess *doesn't answer but keeps on sewing.*

Hannah   Ah, don't be like that. She just rattled you with that trick is all.

Bess   What would you know about it? You were spark out. It's nothing to do with that. I'm just – I'm telling you Hannah, that woman is poison.

Hannah   How'd you figure that? We've never had it this good before.

Bess   She's out for herself, alright? She's not on your side, just remember that. Second there's a bit of work needs doing, she's nowhere to be seen.

Hannah   She's probably getting us money. Lots of money.

Bess   Better hope so. You're the one stitching her trousers so if she comes back with nothing you'll look a right fool.

Ebi   Besides, it's nice just the three of us. Hard to relax around someone who can't go two minutes with asking if this was your card.

Bess *laughs.* **Ebi** *puts down the tape and stands up.*

Ebi   Right, I'm done. Some of them are too wet, have to wait for them to dry.

Bess   Fancy stitching my coat?

Bess *points to a 6 inch gash in the coat over her left shoulder. The lining is spilling out.* **Ebi** *goes to inspect.*

Ebi   Nah, it's too frayed. If I stitch it up now it'll pull open again within the week. Waste of thread.

Bess   Well if I leave it like this it's gonna get damp.

Ebi   Get a new coat.

Bess   Where?

Hannah   Try the church.

Bess   No, they only just gave us this. You really can't fix it?

Ebi   Not with thread.

Bess   Well think of something else.

Ebi   Like what?

Bess   Use your brain, you dozy prick. You're supposed to be a handy man!

Ebi   I'm an electrician –

Hannah   Were an electrician –

Ebi   I am an electrician, and there's no wires in that coat.

Bess   Christ, no wonder your wife swung at you.

Ebi   Oi!

Bess   Trying to knock a bit of sense in.

Ebi   That's not funny, Bess.

Bess (*patronisingly*)   Ebi, use the tape.

An upset **Ebi** *gets the tape and squats down behind* **Bess,** *tearing of bits of tape and ripping these into smaller strips.* **Bess** *continues to sew.*

Ebi   Sit sill.

Bess *comically freezes and drops the needle. After the quickest beat she whistles* **Hannah** *for a fag.*

Hannah *hands what's left over which* **Bess** *smokes contentedly.* **Bess** *begins to whistle 'Dream a Little Dream of Me'. She whistles the first line which* **Hannah** *recognises and begins to tap her foot. As they begin the second line* **Hannah** *takes over the whistle as* **Bess** *begins to tunelessly sing.* **Bess** *changes the last line of the song to 'Kindly fuck off, Ebi?'*

Hannah *and* **Bess** *enjoy this. As they move into the second verse the whistling stops and they all at start singing, coming in at various points. There are plenty of wrong lyrics and missed notes but the enjoyment is visible.* **Ebi** *joins in until the last line which he fluffs, trying to sing the original. Behind them* **Caz** *enters.*

Ebi (*finshing the jacket*)   Oh brilliant, very clever, very good. You lot are wasted out here. A real bloody talent you got there.

Caz   Isn't this a pretty picture? Look at you.

Bess (*softly*)   Fuck's sake.

Hannah   Alright, Caz?

Caz   Got your little stations, singing a song.

Ebi   How'd you do?

Caz   Well, it was a bit quiet today, if I'm being honest, so only £23 from me.

Ebi   Bloody hell.

Caz   You're welcome.

Bess   We've been sat here stitching your clothes . . . you're welcome.

Caz *puts the money away before sitting next to* **Hannah**.

Caz   And busking apparently. Might want to try somewhere a bit busier.

Hannah   It's just a bit of fun.

Ebi   Anything to pass the boredom. Drives you mad if you're not careful.

Caz   True enough. Singing's a new one though, most people just carry a book.

Ebi   What, you and Barney never had a sing?

Caz   Charlie. Can't say we did.

Ebi   So what did you do?

Caz   I don't know. Played a lot of chess.

Beat and then a large group reaction. This is clearly very funny.

Bess   Ooooo! Hear that?

Hannah   Chess?!

Bess   Christ alive.

Ebi   Bit of the old chess, was it? Bloody Nora.

Caz   Am I missing something?

Bess   Very fancy, was that with a spot of tea?

Hannah   Earl Grey.

Caz   Oh, right. I get it.

Ebi   Cucumber sandwiches?

Hannah   And scones.

Bess   No crust for her ladyship.

Ebi   Course not, not a bloody crust for miles.

Bess   Jesus. I tell you what, in all my time out here I've never seen one person playing chess.

Caz   That's cos you need two.

This deflates the mood a bit. She smiles cruelly, eager to return the humiliation.

Caz   You lot should try it. It's all about strategy and planning, you've got to learn to think ahead and work out what the other person's up to. Can't just go charging in. Not a game for blunt tools. (*Beat.*) So on second thoughts maybe you should give it a miss, Bess.

Hannah *gives a little laugh.*

Bess   I'd be fine.

Caz   You don't know a thing about it, do you?

Beat.

Hannah   So, how was it today?

Caz   Fine. You?

Hannah   S'alright.

Ebi   Whereabouts were you?

Caz   Tottenham Court Road, Soho area.

Hannah   Any luck?

Caz   Some. Not the easiest place to do it. But I tell you, funniest thing happened on the way back.

Ebi   Oh yeh?

Caz   Yeh. I was coming back here and thought I'd stop by the Peregrine Shelter. Just put my head in for a brew and that, but when I got there, the place was absolute chaos. Chocka.

Hannah   With people?

Caz   Yeh, did you see them?

Hannah   No.

Caz   There must've been seventy-odd people crammed in. I couldn't move.

Bess   Why?

Caz   Well I thought you'd have known about it.

Bess   'Bout what?

Caz   Apparently they were giving away unused bedding. Duvets and pillows and that. It was all part of this big donation and they couldn't store them in the shelter so they just gave them all away at once.

Bess   What?

Hannah   Did you get one?

Caz   No chance. They'd all gone when I got there.

Ebi   What, all of it?

Caz   Yeh.

Hannah   Shit.

Bess (*shocked*)   Why didn't we know?

The group are clearly more upset by this news than **Caz** *expected, putting her on the back foot. The good mood from before is gone.*

Caz   Search me, that was the first I heard about it.

Bess   But why didn't someone tell us?

Caz   Like who?

Bess   Someone from the shelter. We're on their list. They're supposed to let us know about stuff like this. About giveaways. Otherwise it's not fair, it's not right.

Ebi   People are supposed to pass it on.

Bess (*to* **Hannah**)   Did you know?

Hannah   No. No one said anything to me.

Ebi   Oh, Jesus.

Caz   Well that's what happens if you live tucked away under an arch, people forget. Why would they tell you?

Bess (*furious*)   Cos we're supposed to be a fucking community!

Caz   Alright, chill out.

Quick beat.

Bess *turns on* **Caz**.

Bess   Who was there?

Caz   Eh?

Bess   Who got stuff?

Caz   I don't know.

Bess   You been here three weeks, must've recognised someone. Come on, who got a cover?

Ebi   Bess, maybe just leave it.

Caz   Why're you lot so worked up? It's just a duvet.

Bess (*pointing to* **Hannah**)   How d'you think she does in the cold? Eh? Look at the size of her. And all she's got is some knackered old sleeping bag on a bit of cardboard. It's not just a duvet, it might be the fucking difference.

Ebi   If they've all gone, Bess, what can we do?

Bess   No. If they're giving them out then we should've got one, so who did you see?

Beat. **Caz** *laughs.*

Hannah   Caz?

Caz (*thinking*)   Bloody hell. Uh, I don't know – those two lads with the Staffy. Used to hang out near West Square Gardens. Saw them with a cover. (*To* **Ebi**.) You know them.

Ebi   Matt and Ali?

Caz   Why not.

Bess   The ones who tried to sell us a puppy?

Caz That's them. What are you going to do about it? Complain?

Beat.

Bess *gets up and strides off.*

Ebi Bess!

Hannah Oh shit.

Caz What you doing?

Ebi Bess, don't be – Bess!

He jumps up as if to go with her but his courage fades before he can exit. He shouts after her one last time before returning to the middle.

Ebi Bollocks!

Hannah That's not good.

Caz Where's she off to?

Ebi Where'd you think?

Caz What the – she knows they've got a dog, right?

Ebi That's what I'm worried about.

Hannah Never stopped her before.

Ebi Maybe she won't find them. Where did they go?

Caz They're right outside Southwark Station, Ebi, she'll find them the second she gets on the main road.

Ebi Well, good to see you're right behind her.

Caz Hey, if she wants to go and lose some fingers over a blanket then that's her choice. Nothing to do with me.

Hannah Why didn't you get one?

Caz Get what?

Ebi A cover. Why didn't you get one?

Caz Already told you, it was chaos.

Ebi   So? You should have queued. Should've stuck it out.

Caz   Look, by the time I got there it had all gone.

Ebi   So you came back with nothing?

Caz   I came back with £23, when's the last time you did that? There were loads of people there before me, loads, so don't you two start having a go.

Conflict over, the group settle back down, **Hannah** *and* **Ebi** *concerned,* **Caz** *trying to restore order. After a pause:*

Caz   I mean, we can get a duvet.

Hannah   Really?

Caz   Course.

Ebi   Going to pull one out of a hat are you?

Beat. **Caz** *paces.*

Caz   I tell you, she's kicking up a right mess here. All she's going to do is come back with nothing, piss them off and then what? We'll have two people who want to get back at us.

Hannah   You think?

Caz   I know.

Hannah   Jesus. She's always been like that. Can't control herself, that's the trouble.

Ebi   You can bloody talk.

Hannah   Well at least I don't go getting into fights. What happens when she comes back all busted up? We got to take care of her, that's selfish that is.

Caz   And dangerous. What happens if she gets sick?

Hannah   Exactly.

Caz   And if she carries on like that it'll be the ruin of this place. You can't just go screaming and shouting every time something goes wrong. Sometimes you need brains, a bit of subtlety.

Ebi Easy for you to say when you're on your own, you can move on any time you like. It's harder when you're looking after a group, and staying in one place. Everyone knows where you are. You reckon we got all this stuff easy? That no one ever fancied it? The amount of times people have come in here, looking for what we've got and left with nothing. And it's all because of Bess, cos she doesn't let it happen. You're right bloody quick to forget that, aren't you, Han? Where were you last time someone tried to rob us?

Hannah Hiding in the tent.

Ebi Exactly.

Hannah Next to you.

Quick beat.

Ebi I don't pretend to be perfect. But at least I recognise what she does for us.

Caz Christ, you just can't see the wrong in her, can you? I can, and she's playing you two for fools.

Ebi You need people like Bess when you're . . . here.

Caz You ever think maybe that's why no one tells you about what's going on at the shelters? Are you surprised no one wants to help out the pisshead troll under the arches who wants to throw punches every time things don't go her way? No, you don't need people like her.

Behind **Caz,** **Bess** *returns with the look of someone who's just dispensed a great deal of violence. Her nose is bleeding, as are her knuckles. In her hand is a carrier bag with two duvets inside.* **Caz** *is unaware of* **Bess**'s *re-entrance and carries on talking.*

Caz Her acting like Superman doesn't help you lot, it doesn't get you ahead and it sure as hell doesn't get you a fucking duvet!

Bess, having heard the last bit of this, drops the heavy bag with a loud thump right behind Caz, who leaps up, shocked by the sound. The sight of a post-fight Bess stuns the group who take a second to realise what she's done.

*There is a pause as **Bess** stares at **Caz** before she moves off, limping slightly, to her tent, taking off her coat as she walks.*

Ebi   What happened? Did the dog . . .?

Bess *doesn't answer, but keeps moving.*

*Before she goes into the tent she stops, turns and begins moving back towards **Caz**. The tension rises. **Caz** stiffens as **Ebi** and **Hannah** prepare to intervene. **Bess** stops just short of **Caz**, thinks hard and then says:*

Bess   Uh . . . pawns, kings, check. Knew I remembered something.

She turns. Lights snap down.

Scene Four

*The camp, three days later. **Hannah** has gone. **Caz** sits calmly as **Bess** and **Ebi** try to work out where she might be.*

Bess   Oh, fucking hell, Ebi, why did you do that?!

Ebi   She asked me.

Bess   She asked you what exactly?

Ebi   She asked me if I knew where you kept all the papers from the council and I said they were in the top of your bag.

Bess   She's never once wanted a look, why's she so interested now?

Ebi   Said she wanted to know more about what was going on with the house and that, the application.

Bess (*looking at* **Caz**)   Oh Jesus.

Ebi   What's the harm in that? She can't even read them.

Bess   She'll find someone who can.

Ebi   Why's that a problem?

Bess   Well – she might get ideas.

Caz   Thought you were helping her, Bess.

Bess   It's a slow process. That's not my fault.

Ebi   She'll come back, you don't walk away from a house.

Bess   It's been three days.

Caz   Missing that money?

Bess   No. I just care, that's all.

Caz   Oh, right. Well, maybe she just got a bit scared when she heard what those lads said they're gonna do. Didn't want to get mixed up in it.

Bess   What, Matt and Ali? Don't be soft. It's just a cover.

Caz   Their cover.

Bess   Yeh, well they know where we are, so if they want it back they can come and get it.

Caz   That's exactly what they're going to do, from what I've heard.

Bess *waves her away and turns back to* **Ebi**.

Bess   What did Joe say when you spoke to him?

Ebi   Said he'd seen Hannah two nights ago at the day centre in Hackney.

Bess   And what was she doing?

Ebi   Dunno do I? Washing her clothes I imagine, cup of tea. Get away from it for a bit.

Bess   Then what?

Ebi   He saw her queuing outside the Crisis shelter that night.

Bess   And she got in?

Ebi   He thinks so. Didn't see her milling around outside.

Bess   Ok, ok. So she got in Thursday. Then what?

Ebi   Not so lucky on Friday. Joe said she turned up late, looking a bit haggard, was asking about for some spice, he reckons they took it off her the night before.

Bess   Course they did. Can't walk into a bloody shelter with that shit on you, bet she asked for a light.

Ebi   After that Joe said he saw her walking away with some bloke.

Bess   Who?

Ebi   No idea.

Caz   Reckon he can read, Bess?

Bess   Piss off. Suppose you know nothing about this?

Caz   Me? No, no. But I think it's good she's taking an interest in her own life. This way she'll get to see all the hard work you've put in for her, then she'll come right back. At least, you better hope she does. Less than £7 today wasn't it? Bet that squat's looking a bit more appealing now.

Bess   Piss off.

Ebi   We can't go, what happens if she comes back?

Caz   Trust me, Ebi, the second she gets someone to read those papers she'll never be coming back here again.

Ebi   Why not?

Caz   Ask Bess.

Bess   She'll be back, mark my words. Soon as she remembers all we do for her and gets a taste of what life's like out there she'll come crawling. She owes us, this is just some kid acting out –

Hannah *enters from behind* **Bess** *who turns last minute and is caught with an almighty punch from* **Hannah** *that sends her sprawling and creates chaos in the camp. Everyone jumps up to get between the two women.*

Hannah   You bitch!

She wriggles free of **Ebi** *and manages to give the hunched-over* **Bess** *a kick in the ribs.* **Bess** *goes down again.*

Caz   Whoa!

Ebi   Jesus Christ, Hannah! What are you doing?

Hannah   You slag, you piece of shit!

Ebi   What's wrong with you?

He is struggling to restrain her. **Hannah**'s *rage suddenly turns on him, hand cocked, ready to swing.*

Hannah   Get off me! Did you know? Did you?

Ebi   Know what?

Hannah   Answer me!

Ebi   Know what? Jesus, Hannah, what are you talking about? You can't just come in here and –

Hannah   Shut up. Did you know?

Ebi (*cowering*)   I don't know what you're talking about! I don't know what you're – Please, I don't know!

Hannah *turns once more to* **Bess** *who is still recovering.*

Hannah   Not eligible am I? Not able to register in Southwark am I?

Bess   Now look, Hannah, it's not a simple –

Hannah   You got the letter six months ago. I've been here waiting, and begging and you knew!

Bess   Hannah –

Hannah   Why didn't you tell me?

Beat.

Bess   It's complicated –

Hannah *rushes at* **Bess***, who's managed to get to her feet, and clips her one more time before* **Ebi** *intervenes.* **Bess** *stays on her feet.*

Hannah   Get off me!

Bess   You know, one more of those and I'm going to start swinging back.

Hannah   Fuck you! You knew I wasn't going to get anything.

Ebi   What do you mean? You're getting a house.

Hannah   There's no house. There's not even an application. And she knew.

Ebi   What?

Hannah   When we met she took me to the council to register but I couldn't fill in any of the forms so they let Bess sort it out for me. Three weeks later we went back and she picked up a letter that said I wasn't eligible in this borough, only you didn't tell me that, did you?

Ebi   What's she on about?

Hannah   You told me it was a slow process, to sit tight, to keep going out everyday and bringing in the money just cos old pricks like you two can't get any!

Ebi   Bess?

Bess   It's not like that, it's not like that at all.

Caz   Give up.

Beat.

Bess   Didn't we do things for you? Didn't we care for you?

Hannah   Shut up.

Ebi   So there's no housing list?

Caz   No.

Ebi   So – so what have I been waiting for?

Caz   Ask Bess.

Bess   I kept you safe. Both of you. Showed you where to get the money.

Hannah   Only cos you couldn't.

Bess   Sounds like a fair trade to me. You bring in the cash, and we stop you getting fucked seven ways from Sunday.

Hannah   Bullshit!

Bess   Really? How was your time without us, petal? Can't help but realise you don't have none of your stuff. Blow away did it? What happened to all that money you're so good at getting? Spend it all on that shit you smoke? Or maybe you didn't have enough in the first place and that bloke you went home with was just helping you out. Nice of him. Cup of tea and a soft pillow was it? Yeh, that's why you're back here. Cos the rest of the world was so fucking good to you.

Hannah   Shut your mouth.

Bess   See how hard it is out there without this? Without me?

Hannah*'s rage is fading into tears.*

Beat.

We could have moved around, tried other boroughs for a house.

Bess   Oh, now who's lying? Bet you'd like that, moving around wherever you fancy with us taking care of you.

Hannah   What?

Bess   Go on, tell the truth.

Hannah   I don't know what –

Bess   No council in the country is going to help you, because you've already been housed. When were you going to tell us that, Little Miss Perfect?

Beat.

Hannah   What do you mean?

Bess   Says it right there in that letter you're holding, only you're too thick to read it. Sounds like when you got away from that nasty step-daddy of yours those kind folks at the social services sorted a place out for you.

Caz   Oh, shit.

Ebi   You've already been housed?

Hannah   No.

Bess   Yeh. They got you a temporary spot and you were on the list for a proper council house. See, they're very good at sorting that when you're young and vulnerable. Bit harder for us, what was it Ebi? Old pricks. They got you a spot, didn't they? Go on, tell everyone.

Beat.

Hannah   It was – it was a box! Just a box in some part of town I'd never been to before. There wasn't even anything in it, no chairs or nothing they just – just left me on my own there. I thought I was going to lose it, going to crack, I needed help and my friends and –

Bess   So what did you do?

Beat.

Ebi   What did you do, Han?

Hannah   I left.

Ebi   Oh, no.

Bess   Yes you did.

Hannah (*frantic*)   I wasn't right! I didn't have anything and they just dropped me there. No help, no one to talk to, nothing. So I . . . so I left. That doesn't mean they don't have to help me. I'm better now, I've got . . . stuff, I got you lot.

Bess   Was it your place?

Beat.

Hannah   Yeh.

Bess   And you left?

Hannah   Yeh.

Bess   Then they don't owe you a thing.

Hannah   What?

Bess   They've done their bit, they've helped you once, but you walked away. You are what they call 'intentionally homeless', it's your own fault. And no council in this country is going to spend one penny on some no good, stoned-up, runaway who's already fucked their chances. When were you going to tell us that then, girlie?

Hannah   Shut up! You used me.

Bess   And you used us.

Hannah   I didn't know.

Ebi   Oh, Hannah.

Hannah   Ebi, I didn't . . .

She moves towards **Caz**.

Hannah   Is it true?

Caz   If you walked away then yeh.

Bess   She can't magic you out of this one.

Beat. **Hannah** *stares frantically at the letter, willing herself to understand it. Evenutally she scrunches it up and screams her frustration, curling up centre stage.*

Hannah   What's the point? I mean, what's the fucking point?

She starts skinning up.

Bess   That won't help.

Hannah   I swear to God, if you talk to me again I will – I'll – I will . . .

Bess *falls silent.* **Hannah** *is crying.*

Hannah   It's not fair. I needed help, not a room. My family treated me like an animal, my step-dad fucks me, my friends, boyfriends, they all fuck me, my school fucks me, I finally get away and the social services fuck me. Then you (*Bess*) fuck me, then you (*Ebi*) fuck me, those twats at the shelter fuck me and then there's someone outside waiting to fuck me as well. Only person in the world who hasn't fucked me is you (*Caz*), might as well get it over with. I'm going to spend my life begging for 20p pieces and end up like that bitch (*Bess*), so what's the point?

From her slumped position on the floor she looks pleadingly up to **Caz** *who has been watching from the sides.*

Hannah   Can you help me? Please. I've got no one, no one to help –

Bess   We helped.

Ebi   Shut up, Bess.

Bess   What?

Ebi   Just shut up!

Beat.

Hannah   I've got no one, no one who can help me fix this. Can you talk to someone, like, at the council or something?

Can you tell them it was just a mistake and I'm better and get me a second chance? Please, I need them to give me a place, I need it. Please help me. I've got no one else to ask.

Beat.

Caz (*softly at first*)   See, this is your problem, Hannah, it's that you ask. You keep asking for help. But the council won't help you cos they don't have enough and they don't really care. So you go around asking people for help. And if that don't work you find some charity that'll give you a hot dinner once a month. But all they're doing, all any of them are doing, is giving you is just enough so you can make it to tomorrow and ask again. Why bother? We're surrounded by complete monsters, and you're asking them for help. These people who walk past us all day will happily send £10 a month to Oxfam or whatever it is to buy someone a blanket, but you could be freezing to death right in front of them and they'll walk past you. Tell their mates that they didn't have any change or they were worried what you'd spend it on, but d'you know why they walk past? It's because if they're pushed, when it really comes down to it, they'll say it's your own fault, that you deserve this. Do you?

Hannah   No.

Caz (*to* **Ebi**)   Do you?

Ebi   No.

Caz (*flaring up*)   No, I don't either. I don't think any of us deserve this. You shouldn't have to rely on people like her (*Bess*) to stay safe. You shouldn't have to hide away under the arches cos we know that the same people who walk past in the day will kick us, piss on us and set our bags on fire when night comes. Why are you asking those people for help? Why do you smile and say 'God bless' when they ignore you? Doesn't that make you sick? Doesn't that burn you inside?

Hannah   Yeh.

Caz   So stop asking and start demanding! There's three of us here. Reckon any one of the thousand-odd people who pass you each day remembers what you look like? Knows your name? If we're not protected by the rules then why the fuck should we follow them? Don't you want a bit of pride in your life? A day off from begging for help?

Ebi   Yeh.

Caz   Hannah?

Hannah   Yeh.

Caz   Well then, let's have it, let's take it. We can set off any time you want, find an empty place, get the door open and it's ours.

Bess   Hannah, it's not that simple. If it were we'd all be doing it. Listen, we can go back –

Ebi   I don't think anyone here needs to listen to you, Bess.

Hannah *stares at* **Bess** *then looks up to* **Caz**.

Hannah   I just want . . . something nice in my life.

Caz   I know.

Hannah   I want to live like a normal person for a few hours.

Ebi   Me too. A break from . . . this.

Hannah   And her.

Ebi   Yeh, and her.

Bess   Ebi.

Caz   Fine. Let's go.

Bess   What about me?

Caz   Way I see it this is your fault, you're why they've been waiting here for nothing. So you're staying here and watching our stuff.

Bess   No I'm not.

Hannah   What if she does a runner?

Bess   I'm not staying anywhere.

Caz   She won't.

Hannah   Wouldn't put it past her.

Bess   Ebi?

Ebi   Don't look at me, you snake.

Bess   Oi!

Caz   S'alright, Bess here needs us now, don't you, Bess?

Bess   Oh, fuck you.

Caz   See? She's not going anywhere, cos she's not got anywhere to go. Whose group is it, Bess? (*Nothing.*) Come on.

They leave, **Bess** *remains.*

Lights.

Scene Five

The camp. **Bess** *sits alone, bored and waiting. After a while* **Hannah** *enters, bouncier and more authoritative than before. She stops as she enters, slowly moving into the middle.*

Bess   Just you?

Hannah   They've gone to get some food and that.

Bess   I see. Reckon I'll be coming on one of these little jaunts any time soon?

Hannah   Nope. You're not done apologising for what you did to me.

Bess   I didn't do anything you wouldn't have done to me. And I think I've apologised plenty, two weeks stuck here is more than enough.

Hannah   Well it's what I think that matters.

Bess   Is it?

Hannah   Now it is, yeh.

Bess   I see, no need for me anymore.

Hannah   Well done, you're catching on.

Bess *chuckles and looks at* **Hannah**.

Bess   You know I'm not sure I recognise you anymore, girlie.

Hannah   Don't call me that.

Bess   Girlie.

Hannah   Shut up.

Bess   Make me.

Beat.

See, you're all big and brave when your new mate's around, but just remember there are certain times, times when we're alone, time like this for example, where I could snap you over my leg like a twig.

Hannah *takes a step backwards.*

Hannah   Why don't you?

Bess   Cos –

Hannah   Cos you need our food and our money and we need someone to watch our stuff while we go have fun.

Bess   You're not wrong.

Hannah   A month without us, and you'd be found frozen to death on a park bench. Course, that's if Matt and Ali don't get you first. And the dog.

Bess *looks over.* **Hannah** *smiles, happy to have landed.*

Hannah   They've been asking around about you. Caz says if they come here we should just let them at you.

Bess   Then you'll lose all your stuff.

Hannah   It's you they got a problem with.

Bess   What you think they'll come here and ask nicely who owns what? You lot are in this one with me, girlie.

Hannah   Well then maybe we should just kick you out, get rid of the problem.

Bess   All the thanks I get.

Hannah   No one asked you to jump them.

Bess   I didn't jump them, they saw me coming from up the street.

Hannah   Yeh, well apparently Alis a black belt in karate so –

Bess   Is that what that was? I thought he went down like a sack of shit, but I had no idea he learnt it from a grand master. (*She sighs deeply.*) I'm so tired of this.

Hannah   Funny. I never felt better.

Pause.

Bess   Well, enjoy it while it lasts.

Hannah   What's that mean?

Bess   Way you're carrying on, stealing from shops, robbing out of garden sheds, smashing car windows – where were you tonight?

Hannah   Cinema.

Bess   Ha! It'll catch up with you soon enough, and then what? I don't reckon Her Holiness sticks around long enough to find out. Remember what happened last time you tried to go it alone?

Hannah   It's different now.

Bess   Oh yeh?

Hannah   Yeh, I know more, more about the world, and people and how to get what I need.

Bess   You got all that in two weeks?

Hannah   I'm a quick learner.

Bess   No you're not. You're one knock in the head away from retarded.

Hannah   Fuck you. I learnt pretty quick how to deal with pricks like you. I'm smarter than you think.

Bess   If you were smart you wouldn't be out here.

Hannah   Caz is smart, she's out here.

Bess   And that doesn't make you think? That doesn't itch a bit? You don't wonder how fucked up someone has to be if they can count cards and pull £20 out of their arse whenever they feel like it and still end up here? First bit of trouble you run into, first bit, I don't care if it's the police or Bruce Lee and his mutt, she will disappear.

Hannah   Well, she is magic.

Bess   She is not fucking magic!

Hannah   She is. Yesterday in Leicester Square she did that mind-reading trick she done to Ebi and these tourists were so impressed they gave her £20, no lie –

Bess   What does that prove? –

Hannah   And then, last week we were having a poke around the back of this shop, trying to see a way in but the gates at the back were padlocked. It's the middle of the night, I'm getting the spooks so I say 'let's just go', Caz takes one look at the lock, gives it a squeeze and the whole thing flies open. What d'you call that?

Bess   Rusty locks.

Hannah   You weren't complaining when we brought all that food back.

Bess   A box of Doritos? If you were going in for robbery I'd have rather had the money.

Hannah   Yeh, well we couldn't get into the main bit.

Bess   All out of magic was she? Needed to drink the tears of a dove before she could perform another miracle?

Hannah   No, it was just locked from the inside.

Beat.

Bess   David Blaine would've got it open.

Hannah   Wouldn't.

Bess   He fucking would. And he'd have found us all a squat by now.

Hannah   It's not that easy.

Bess   That's what I said, remember? But I was told 'how hard can it be to find a boarded-up house in London?'.

Hannah   That's easy, but we don't want one we share. We want our own one, our own spot, and that takes time.

We hear approaching voices.

Course if you've got a problem with how it's all going then why don't you bring it up?

Nothing.

Didn't think so.

*Enter **Ebi** and **Caz** carrying bags full of cans and half-empty popcorn boxes.*

Caz   Well hello there, Bess.

Bess   Alright? Good day was it? Ebi?

Ebi (*coldly, walking past her*)   Bess.

Bess   Oh I forgot, this dog's got a new leash.

Ebi   Just leave me out of it.

Bess   Don't know why you're having a grump.

Hannah   Well it weren't just me you fucked over.

Bess   You know the plan was to force our way in with you? To get in the house. He's not exactly innocent.

Caz   He's better than you.

Beat.

Bess   I hear you lot went to the pictures.

Caz   Can't imagine what gave you that idea.

Bess   And I see you chose to spend our money on popcorn.

Ebi   We didn't spend a penny. Picked this lot up as we were leaving. The things people waste.

Bess   Hold up. You actually went into a film?

Hannah   Oh yes.

Bess   Like into the seats and that?

Caz   Yep.

Bess *is shocked.*

Bess   How was it?

Hannah   Incredible. Wasn't it, Ebi?

Ebi   It was amazing. We were just standing around, getting a bit chilly and I saw this poster for a film so I said, off-hand like, 'that looks good', 'let's find out' says Caz and next thing you know we're stood behind the Camden Odeon on Inverness Street, looking up the fire escape. Old magic hands here has a quick fiddle on the gates and we're in, straight up the stairs, quick look around and sneak into the back row of the first screen we found.

Bess   You didn't.

Hannah   We did.

Ebi   And it was bloody wonderful. Warm and quiet. No one knows who you are in a place like that. You're just a person watching a film.

Bess   Jesus Christ, can't remember the last time I saw a movie. What was it?

Ebi   Eh?

Bess   What was the film?

Ebi   Oh, no idea. I slept through the whole thing, best kip I've had in years.

Bess   You didn't watch it?

Ebi   No.

Caz   I did. It was shit. Wasn't even a film, it just was some documentary about climate change.

Bess   Why didn't you move?

Hannah   Didn't want to risk getting caught.

Caz   Plus Ebi was already spark out.

Bess   So you just watched it?

Hannah   Yeh.

Bess   And?

Caz   Well, the long and the short of it is things aren't looking too good.

Bess   Oh no?

Caz   Apparently global warming's out of control and if we don't get our act together sharpish we'll lose the polar bear, the mountain gorilla and the entire Amazon rainforest in the next twenty years.

Bess Right.

Caz Yeh.

Beat. **Bess** *thinks.*

Bess Sorry but who gives a fuck?

Collective agreement.

Hannah That's what I said.

Bess I mean who, in their right mind, gives a fuck about a mountain gorilla.

Hannah Yeh. There was this one woman a few rows in front of me who sobbed through the whole thing, shaking her head, tutting. And at the end of it she actually stood up to give it a clap.

Bess What?

Hannah I could've kicked her head in.

Caz It was unbelievable.

Hannah Felt like telling her if you're sleeping in a fucking tent, global warming can't come soon enough, love.

Ebi Bet she was one of those people, right, who when you ask for help make a point of coming over just so they can say 'I already give to charity'.

Collective agreement. Laughter, cans going around. They're enjoying the impersonations.

Hannah Yeh. Like we should be grateful, like that makes it all ok.

Caz Yeh, yeh, on behalf of the great unwashed thank you so much for all those steak dinners we've been having.

Ebi Yeh, exactly, thanks for the one night a year there's space in the hostel.

Bess Thanks for all those studies you help fund. I'm growing fat on studies –

Hannah   I'm sweating with all those studies.

Caz   Now please, go in peace, and with our blessing, to cry yourself to sleep over some fucking tiger!

Bess   Not as bad as the ones who sit down with you though.

Agreement.

Ebi   Oh my God.

Hannah   Men. They're always men.

Caz   Yeh.

Hannah   It's unbelivable. I've never once had a woman try to sit next to me, but at least twice a week (*affecting a do-gooder voice*), 'Hey pal, hey mate, d'you mind if I sit with you?'

They enjoy the impression.

Yeh, I do fucking mind. I don't sit next to him when he's at work, chat about how 'life's tough sometimes'.

Caz   Imagine. 'I actually once had a friend who was an accountant, so I know what you're going through. It's not right.'

Bess   'Stay stong, mate.'

Ebi   'Chin up, friend.'

Caz   'Here's a sandwich.'

Hannah   Ah, get fucked.

Ebi   Or when you don't want the sandwich.

Bess   Oh, yeh.

Ebi   I hopped the tube a few months back and was walking down the carriages, y'know, asking if anyone had any food. Got a Mars bar, apple, all good, then got to this one woman who pulls out a tuna sandwich. I could smell it the second she got it out, had oil stains all round the packet and that.

(*He shudders theatrically.*) So I said, 'No thanks, I don't like tuna'.

Caz *tutts.*

Ebi   She honestly looked like I'd spat on her. 'Well I never!' Everyone's mortified apparently and suddenly no one's got anything. I don't like tuna. I fucking hate it. Why am I not allowed to feel like that? What, because I don't pay rent I've got to eat anything they give me? I'm not fucking livestock.

Collective agreement.

How do they all get like that? Or like that one at the cinema. How can they get so twisted in their heads that they'll mist up over some bear they'll never see, in some place they'll never go, but I'm right bloody here. (*Beat.*) Y'know I might not be a model citizen, but for most of my life I paid tax in this country, I'm a part of this society and I reckon I matter at least as much as some fucking bear. (*Beat.*) I never acted that way to people when I had a home and that . . . I didn't ignore them.

Caz   Don't be a twat, Ebi. Of course you did.

Ebi   No, I –

Caz   And if you got lucky on the scratch cards, you'd be ignoring us again tomorrow.

Ebi (*sighing*)   I – Yeh. I just – I don't know how people can get like that if – If they know, y'know?

Bess   Well they probably don't want to spend too long thinking about it. It could so easily have been them, too easily, that if they really stop to think about it they'll go bananas. I don't blame them.

Hannah   That's bollocks, that is. Not all just bad luck. Some people deserve it.

Beat.

Bess   You mean me?

Hannah   What goes around, comes around.

Bess   Ah, Hannah. You don't know what you're talking about.

Hannah   I know that if my dad had been a priest I wouldn't be here –

Bess   He wasn't a priest –

Hannah   I wouldn't do things like you done. Yeh, some people do deserve it. To go from there to here –

Bess   Where's 'there', exactly?

Hannah   Having someone in your life who's – who's like a good person. I never had that.

Caz   Me neither.

Hannah   And if I had, there's no chance I'd be here.

Bess   Really?

Hannah   Yeh, none.

Bess   How can you – ? Right, yeh, my old man was a lovely bloke.

Hannah   There you are.

Bess   My mum was a prick.

Caz (*sarcastically*)   Oh, I see.

Ebi   Should've just stayed with your dad, problem solved.

Bess   Ebi, do me a favour and just shut up, will you? Go back to being a martyr.

Beat.

My dad was a nice guy, my mum wasn't, they divorced when I was twelve, and got shared custody. Not my choice. And over the years she made it very difficult. Always late, changed pick-up spots last minute, y'know, and – Christ, this sounds stupid – it all fell apart when my dad wanted me to get confirmed –

Hannah   Bloody hell –

Bess   You asked, alright? He wanted me to get confirmed but I was coming from hers and she was an hour late. So I wasn't changed, my hair was all over the shop and he was just – he going to lose it, which is not something a twelve-year-old can really get. So he drags me into the back of the church and starts trying to get me to change but I must've been messing about so eventually he loses his patience, and just tries to force the robe-thing over my head. (*Beat.*) People start looking around to see what the fuss is about and, in the struggle we're having, I swung out, and scratched him down the side of his face . . . and he just snapped, hit me right back, just a slap like, but I fell into one of the benches, cracked my head and – y'know? Never even shouted at me before but . . . It goes to court, I tell the truth, he goes to jail, my mum's deemed unfit, I end up in foster care and from there to here, it's really not that far. If she was on time, I'm not here. I'm baking cakes and watching *Corrie*. Now, do you want to tell me which part of that was my fault?

Beat.

Caz   Should've put the robe on.

Bess *gives a little laugh and shrugs.*

Bess   Yeh, shoulda. Just make a mistake. Same way you (*Hannah*) made a mistake leaving that house of yours. But that weren't your fault, was it?

Hannah   No.

Bess   No. Just a mistake. But right now I seem to be paying for mine more than most, and that's not fair, it it?

Caz   Well you fucked up more than most.

Bess   I thought the whole idea of this 'change' or whatever it is, is that we'd stop being angry at each other, and start being angry at them. Wasn't it?

Ebi   Yeh, she's got a point.

Bess   You lot are out there every day, asserting yourselves, taking food and that, and I'm sat here bored out my mind just because –

Hannah   Because you lied.

Bess   I made the best of a bad situation. I'm not the one who says you can't have a house. I'm not the one who wrote you off. I'm the one who brought you here, got you a tent, got you a cover for Christ sake.

Hannah   With my money.

Bess   It was someone else's money, you just got it off of them. Lord knows where you'd have spent it otherwise. I made this place, you can't just kick me out of it.

Caz *chuckles*.

Ebi   She does have a point, Hannah.

Bess   Thank you, Ebi.

Pause. **Hannah** *looks to* **Caz**.

Hannah (*to* **Caz**)   What do you think?

Bess   Who gives a fuck what she thinks /

Hannah   Shut it /

Caz   Here we go /

Bess   Fucking snake /

Hannah   Oi! You want back in, we've all got to get along. Alright?

Bess *nods.* **Hannah** *stands.*

Hannah   Now. You going to be a part of this group?

Bess   Yeh.

Hannah   And are you really, properly sorry for lying to me?

Bess   Yes.

Ebi   And me?

Bess   Yes.

Hannah   You going to help us find a squat?

Bess   Yeh.

Caz   You going to get rid of me, first chance you get?

Beat.

Bess   No.

Hannah *looks to* **Caz**, *then shrugs.*

Hannah   Cool.

Bess   Cool? Cool what? What are you saying?

Caz   Jesus, give it a bit of swagger, girl.

She strides across the stage, grabbing a box of popcorn on the way, until she is stood in front of **Bess**.

Caz   Right, by the power vested in me by – get on your knees, Bess.

Beat. **Bess** *kneels.*

Caz   Good girl – Now, by the power vested in me by the despicable Southwark Council, I hereby declare you Bess Never-bothered-to-learn-your-second-name, officially forgiven. And we give you this crown as a symbol of your re-entry. Arise as the twat you are, but a forgiven twat, and welcome to your new life.

She empties the popcorn over **Bess**'s *head and rests the box on top like a crown.* **Ebi** *cheers and applauds.* **Caz** *joins in.*

Ebi   Give her a clap, Hannah.

Hannah *does so.*

Ebi   That's good, that's nice. We're all back together again. We shouldn't be fighting.

Bess   Yeh, let's have a fresh start.

Caz grabs a crate from beside one of the tents used as a stool and stands on it like a soap-box.

Caz (*theatrically*)   Exactly, with a new philosophy. We are now a united group who will not beg and ask for help, who won't live under arches like rats. We are now a group that, together, will start to live the lives we want.

Hannah   Yeh.

Caz   If we're hungry, if we need food, we get it.

Collective agreement, pressure rising.

Wanna go to the films? We go.

Agreement.

Want a house so we can be warm, and safe? We fucking take it!

Big cheers. Fever pitch.

I promise you that this time next month we're going to be inside four walls and making our own lives.

Hannah   And if anyone tells us we can't have it, or that we don't deserve it, we'll kick their fucking heads in.

Ebi   Yeh!

Bess   People should be scared of us.

Caz   Damn right.

Bess   They should know that you can't cut us loose, can't just chuck us out of their world.

Ebi   Yeh, they should feel that every road they walk down might have one of us waiting on it ready to wham! To take what they don't think we should have!

Caz   This is the start of something new, and the next mutherfucker I see who doesn't think I'm worth their time is going to get –

A **Man** *enters dressed in a suit with a backpack on and dragging a suitcase, staring at his phone for directions. He walks across the stage, hurriedly; on the way he flings a coin into the popcorn box* **Hannah** *is holding. He exits. The entire group falls silent. Then:*

Ebi   Caz.

Caz   I know.

Ebi   Caz.

Caz   I know. Shut up and let me think.

Hannah   Do you think he heard us? Do you think he's come to – to get us?

Bess   No.

Hannah   For the cinema.

Bess   Shut up. (*To* **Caz**.) It's after eight.

Caz   That's exactly what I'm thinking.

Hannah   So?

Bess   What do you mean 'so'? Means he's coming back.

Hannah   Why?

Ebi   They gate the car park up after eight. No way through.

Beat.

Hannah   Oh, shit!

Caz *springs into action.*

Caz   How much did he give you?

Hannah *rustles in the box.*

Hannah   £1.

Bess   He had a bag.

Caz   Yeh.

Bess   Like a big bag.

Ebi   Could be clothes.

Caz   Could be a laptop, could be speakers, could be – could be fuck loads of cash, I don't know.

The tension and excitement is sky high.

Ebi   Shit, shit. Are we doing this?

Hannah   Doing what?

Bess   Not in the camp.

Caz   We can move camp.

Ebi   He'll be coming back any second.

Hannah   What are we doing?

Ebi   Just ask him for some money and let him go.

Caz   We'll just end up with another pound. I want what's in his bag, in his pockets!

Hannah   How do we get that?

Bess   We grab him.

Ebi   We don't want to rough up someone who's just got a bag full of paper. He could be some boring bloke with nothing but plastic in his wallet and then we've got to go on the run. Pack this up, leave Southwark, find a spot –

Hannah   We're already looking for –

Caz   Shut the fuck up! Let me think!

Beat. **Hannah** *goes to keep an eye out.*

Caz   Alright. We don't want to mug someone who's got nothing on them but if he's got anything of worth in that bag we're having it. Yeh?

Bess   Yeh.

Ebi   How we going to know?

Caz   Just let me talk to him, I'll find out what he's got.

Hannah   He's coming!

Caz   Just make sure he doesn't leave.

Bess   What if he makes a run for it?

Beat.

Caz   Get him.

Ebi   Right, Hannah, get over here!

Bess   Come on, come on!

Caz   Shhhh!

Hannah, **Ebi** *and* **Bess** *form a screen stage right leaving* **Caz** *in the middle, twitchy and ready. Beat.* **Man** *enters. He's staring at his phone trying to work out where he is; he looks up and sees the group but goes back to his phone. He sighs in frustration and mutters:*

Man   Oh, for fuck's sake.

He holds the phone up, trying to get it to locate itself.

Beat.

Caz   You lost, sir?

Man   I'm fine thanks.

Caz   Trying to get somewhere?

Man   I don't have – I'm fine, really.

Caz *finally starts moving forward.*

Caz   Oh, I'm not after anything, sir, just making a little conversation. Besides, happy to help after that generous donation you just made.

Man *looks up, but says nothing, back to phone.* **Caz** *looks to the group who urge her on.*

Caz   You look like you're off somewhere.

Nothing.

Sir? Are you looking for something?

Man *sighs, gives up on his phone and looks at* **Caz**.

Man   I have a train that's leaving in (*checking watch*) what is now 30 minutes, and I'm trying to get some food before I leave, apparently there's a Pret on Ewer Street.

Caz   Well Ewer Street's just through there.

Man   Yes, I know but I can't get through and now my phone can't work out where I am.

Caz   They gate it after eight, you have to walk round.

Man (*sighing*)   And how long is that going to take?

Ebi   Might be a bit tight, if you've got to get to the station.

Bess   And it's always chocka there.

Man   Brilliant. Just fucking brilliant.

He takes his phone out again. The group are faintly deterred by his aggressive and tense attitude.

Caz   You alright, sir?

Man   I'm fine, I'm just – I was late leaving, I need to eat something and now I don't have time and . . .

He sighs dramatically. **Caz** *slowly withdraws a packet of Doritos from her pocket and offers it to him. He stares.*

Man (*unconvincingly*)   I couldn't.

Caz   We've got loads.

Bess   Whole tent full of them.

Man   Right.

He awkwardly walks forward, takes the bag and retreats a few steps, opens them and starts eating. It calms him down. He sits on top of his suitcase.

Caz   Better?

Man   Yes, thank you, sorry about – sorry – I just haven't had a moment all day and then my blood sugar was getting low and I was rushing and I just – sorry.

Caz   S'alright. Maybe give up on the Pret, sir. Grab yourself something when you head to the station.

Man   Yes, I think – yes.

Beat.

Caz   So, where you off to?

Man *frowns.*

Caz   You're only ten minutes away from the train. Packet of crisps doesn't earn us a conversation?

Beat.

Man   Sorry, no it – I'm visiting my dad.

Caz   Oh yeh?

Man   Well collecting him really.

Caz   That sounds nice.

Man   Not really. Last week he fell down the stairs and cracked his pelvis.

Caz   Oh. I'm sorry.

Man   Yeh. So now I've got to go to his house, to bring him back here so he can stay with me while he recovers.

Caz   I see. Mum not around to help out?

Man   No, she passed a couple of years ago. Took me that long to get him to move, and first thing he does is slip down the stairs. Lucky me.

Caz   Lucky him, couple of weeks being waited on by you, bet it was deliberate.

Man   Ha! More than a couple of weeks, three months until he can even walk again apparently, four at his age.

Caz   You're joking.

Man   'Fraid not.

Caz   And he'll be spending all that time with you?

Man *nods. Eats.*

Caz   You're a good man, aren't you? (*To the group.*) Hear that? He's going to give his old man four months of the hotel treatment while he recovers. How about that then?

Beat.

Bess   You're a saint, sir.

Caz   Isn't he just?

Man   That's very kind of you, (*Checking his watch.*) I should probably –

Caz   And what is it you do, sir? Doctor? Lawyer? Banker?

Man   Oh, I work in education.

Visible slump.

Hannah   Private school?

Bess *stamps hard,* **Hannah** *shuts up.*

Man (*a bit disconcerted*)   Uh, state actually.

Caz   Ah, teacher are you?

Man   Yes, well no, I'm the deputy head.

Caz   Of the whole school?

Man   Yes.

Caz   Wow, very impressive. So young as well.

Man   Well, I work very hard so . . .

Caz   Ah, that's where we went wrong, eh?

Man   Oh, well, I wouldn't – I didn't say that –

Caz   S'alright, sir, just joking. Now you won't want to be missing your train.

She gestures offstage. **Man** *starts moving.*

Man   No, of course. Thank you very much for the crisps.

Caz   You're welcome, we were lucky to talk with such an accomplished young man. Enjoy your trip to – (*As he approaches her she holds out an arm. He's close now, she looks right at him.*) where was it you were going again? I never asked.

Man   Oh, Cambridge.

Caz   Stop it.

Man   Pardon me?

Caz   Your dad lives in Cambridge?

Man (*uncertain*)   Yes.

Caz   Well I only bloody grew up there!

Man   Did you?

Caz   Yeh.

Hannah   Did you?

Caz (*turns nastily*)   Yes, I fucking did.

Hannah   Sorry.

Caz (*back to* **Man**)   So whereabouts is he?

Man   Cambridge.

Caz   Go on, where? Dunheath? Marton? Fairlop?

Man   Oh, I really don't know, it's a new city for me. (*Trying to be helpful.*) He's near the university?

Caz   I remember walking around there as a nipper, looking at all the buildings.

Man   Yes, it's very nice.

Caz   You ever taken your dad for some food at The Coppers?

Man   I'm sorry?

Caz   The Coppers Arms? No? Oh, it's one of the best pubs in the city. Real secret too so it won't be packed with students. Take your old man, you can have a nice meal without some twenty-year-old wiggling her arse in your face. You've got to take him before you bring him back here, he'll love you for ever.

Man   Thought they had to do that.

Caz   You thought wrong, boy.

Awkward laugh.

Anyhow, you gotta take him, and you've got to find out if Matty still works behind the bar. Bet he does, never had any drive that boy, find Matty and tell him Stephanie Broderick says 'Hi'. Watch him, he'll go pale as a ghost. Alright?

Man   Right, thanks for the tip.

He makes to leave. **Caz** *blocks him again.*

Caz   You'll be needing directions!

Man   Oh, I'll get them on my phone.

Caz   What, the same thing that brought you down here? No, no, you'll end up in Glasgow. I'll tell you where it is.

She doesn't stop staring at the **Man**.

Man   Ok.

Caz   Where are you starting from? Which part of town?

Man   I really don't know, I've only been there once.

Caz   Well what's the road name? Maybe I'll know from there.

Man   Uh, (*thinking*) Avery Road.

Caz   Avery road, Avery Road . . . I know the one, just down from the high street?

Man   I –

Caz   Right, so you come out the top, take a right – Wait a sec, might be easier for you to go the other way. Is he at the top or the bottom?

Man   I really don't know, look I've got to get moving –

Caz   Well is he closer to the hairdresser's at like 130, or is he down by the newsagents' at number 3?

Man   I didn't know there was a hairdresser's on –

Caz   Well where is he between 3 and 130? Come on, I'm just trying to get you to say 'hi' to an old friend of mine, I don't exactly get to go home much. Help me out.

Man   He's at number 87.

Beat. **Caz** *smiles.*

Caz   Right. So you come out the top, take a right, straight down the high street about a mile, then it's left at the shopping centre, and it's tucked away there. Simple see?

Man *looks uncomfortable and can't stop looking at* **Caz***.*

Man   Yes.

Caz   What's my friend called?

Man (*quietly*)   Matty.

Caz   That's right, and what's my name?

Man   Uh, Stephanie . . .

Caz   Stephanie Broderick, yeh.

Beat.

Go on then, don't want you missing your train.

Man *walks past them, uncomfortably close. Before he gets to the main group he turns and pulls out his wallet, looking through it for a £5 note.*

Man   Thank you for the crisps.

Unsure of what to do he thinks about giving it to the group or **Caz** *but, in his discomfort, ends up just leaving it on the floor. He goes to leave but bumps into* **Hannah***; he apologises, then hurries off. Pause.* **Hannah** *is nonplussed.*

Bess   Well done, Caz!

Hannah   What the fuck was all that about?

Caz   Shut up.

Hannah   Why didn't we grab him?!

Bess (*to* **Caz**)   Did you get it?

Caz   Yeh.

Hannah   We just let him fucking go!

Bess   That was amazing.

Hannah   Talking all that bollocks about some pub, and since when have you been from Cambridge? Thought you were from Porstmouth.

Bess   Shut up, Hannah!

Beat. **Ebi** *twigs.*

Ebi   Oh, God.

Caz   What?

Ebi   That was – that was great.

Caz   Cheers.

Bess   Sure you got it?

Caz   Yeh.

Bess   Not going to forget?

Caz   No.

Ebi   You genius.

Bess   How we gonna get there?

Caz   Walk it if we have to.

Hannah (*pulling a wallet out of her pocket*)   Well, I don't know what you lot are on about, but at least he was kind enough to leave us this.

Caz   Where did you get that?

Hannah   He put it in his coat pocket after he gave us the note. I just lifted it out again.

Ebi   Jesus Christ.

Caz   Oh, you complete fucking muppet, Hannah!

Hannah   What you talking about?

Bess   Gimme that!

She snatches the wallet and makes to leave.

Caz   No, no. I'll go! He knows me.

She exits with the wallet.

Hannah   What is wrong with you lot?

Bess   What's wrong with you?

Ebi   Use you're brain, Hannah.

Hannah   I don't understand –

Bess   What's he going to do when he realises the last place he had his wallet was with us?

Hannah   Who gives a shit? I thought this whole thing was about us taking stuff.

Ebi   We can take more than his wallet, Han.

Hannah   You what?

Caz *re-enters.*

Ebi   Did you find him?

Caz   Yeh.

Bess   And?

Caz   Seemed fine. Don't ever do that again, Hannah!

Hannah   Sorry.

Bess   How long do you reckon?

Caz   Three days?

Ebi   I'd give it a week.

Caz   Ok.

Bess   Write it down.

Caz   Either of you got a pen?

Ebi   No.

Bess   Well say it again.

Caz   87 Avery Road.

Bess   87 Avery Road.

Ebi, **Bess** *and* **Caz** *start chanting this under their breath to lodge the address.*

Hannah   Sorry, what the fuck is going on? What are you doing? Since when have you been Stephanie? And why were you banging on about your life story to –

Caz   The house, Hannah. I said all that stuff to find out the address of the house.

Beat.

Hannah   Why?

Beat.

Ebi   We've been looking for a place to be.

Hannah (*not getting it*)   Right.

Caz (*slowly*)   We've been looking for a place that no one else's in.

Hannah   But his dad's there.

Bess (*calmly*)   Not for the next four months he's not.

Beat.

Hannah   Oh . . .

Beat. She gets it.

Oh, what?! We can't do that! / That's not right!

The others swarm around her, trying to manage her.

Ebi   Easy, easy /

Bess   Calm down, Hannah /

Caz   Listen to what we're saying /

Ebi   Cool down a bit /

Hannah   I'm not doing that. I'm not doing that!

Caz   Oi, listen! 'If anyone says we can't have it, we kick their heads in.' You just said that.

Bess   We heard you say it.

Hannah   Yeh, when it's one guy!

Ebi   What?

Hannah   When it's one bloke and we're just taking his wallet but – this is a house.

Ebi   So? What's the difference?

Hannah   Well it's a house, isn't it? It's not the same. It's someone's home. It's special.

Bess   How would you know?

Hannah   Can't just kick the door down and take over someone's life.

Caz   Says who?

Hannah   The law.

Ebi   Law also says you can't smoke spice, that you can't nick food, or people's wallets for that matter, law says a lot of things you don't listen to. Ten minutes ago you were screaming and shouting about taking what we're owed. So what's this about?

Beat. **Hannah** *is wavering.*

Hannah   I thought we were just saying all that stuff.

Caz   I wasn't just saying it.

Bess   No, me neither.

Hannah   So we just go to Cambridge and rob some old man's house?

Caz   No, no, no. We live in it first. Picture it, Han, clean sheets, nice beds, baths –

Bess   Probably got some savings stashed away that we can use. Old people always keep some cash.

Ebi   Bet he's got a freezer full of food. Steak and that.

Caz   I'll bet he does too. We can get away from this. Get right. Get back on our feet. Then all we got to do is make sure everything's ready to hop it when the time comes.

Hannah   But what if he comes back?

Ebi   You heard the man. It'll be four months before we need to worry about that.

Hannah   Yeh but what if he comes back early?

Caz   Then we have an encounter.

Beat.

Hannah   What kind of encounter?

Caz   Well, he's fallen down the stairs once already.

Hannah   Eh?

Caz   What's to say it can't happen again?

Beat. **Bess** *breaks the tension*

Bess   Relax, Hannah, he cracked his pelvis, he won't be coming back early.

Hannah   But he will eventually, and when that happens? He'll be coming back to nothing but a stripped-out house. He's an old man.

Caz (*furious*)   Oh for fuck's sake. He's got family. What you on about 'he'll have nothing'? He's spending four months with his son who takes care of him and loves him, and at the end of that he'll still going back to a fucking home! So he loses a few things on the way, so what? He'll survive. Y'know who's really got nothing? You. And now you're about to get something, so don't you dare go soft on me now.

Hannah   But what if he doesn't have anything else and he ends up like us?

Caz   Good. Then he'll have seen this side of life before he pops off.

Hannah   That's not right.

Caz *moves towards* **Hannah**. *Fixes her with a stare.*

Caz   Look at me.

Hannah   I don't want to –

Caz   Look at me.

Hannah *does. Beat.*

Caz   Don't think like that, Hannah.

Ebi   Like what?

Bess   What's she thinking?

Hannah   I'm not thinking anything!

Caz   You don't want to stay behind, trust me.

Bess   Hannah, come on.

Hannah   I wasn't thinking that.

Caz   Yes you were. Do you know what happens if you stay here? Nothing. It would be just be you, and you, Hannah, are not made to be on your own.

Beat.

Hannah   What about you, Ebi, you sure you want to go?

Ebi   Sure I don't want to stay here.

Hannah   Bess?

Bess   Same.

Hannah   But what if it was your dad?

Bess   It's not.

Hannah   Things might change, might get better.

Bess   We've been out here years, Hannah. Things don't get better. They're getting worse.

Caz   Only way things change is if you come with us. We're starting something new and that can lead . . . anywhere. New houses, new councils. This can be a change in your life, Han, a real change, and you wanna let it pass cos we might have to break some eggs along the way? No. We've got a week to get enough money for a train ticket and then we're gone. Only thing for you here is the cold and two lads with a grudge to settle.

Bess   Remember what happened last time you tried to go it alone?

Hannah *nods.*

Ebi   You don't want to be following strange men home just so you can get a place to sleep.

Hannah   Yeh.

She is hunching into herself. **Caz** *takes off her coat and puts it over* **Hannah***'s shoulders, grabbing the lapels and holding her close, maybe doing up the zip, fixing her collar.*

Bess   If you sit around here on your own waiting for things to change then the weather is going to get you long before some street team does.

Ebi   We're a group, Hannah. Like a family.

Caz   Yeh, exactly. He gave you a quid. (*With a flourish* **Caz** *produces the pound coin from behind* **Hannah***'s ear and gives it to her.*) I just gave you my coat. See the difference?

Hannah   Yeh.

Caz   So, are you coming?

Beat.

Hannah   Yeh.

Caz   Good.

Lights snap down.

End.

www.ingramcontent.com/pod-product-compliance
Ingram Content Group UK Ltd.
Pitfield, Milton Keynes, MK11 3LW, UK
UKHW020709280225
455688UK00012B/337